Why Not Me?

Sometimes, We Ask the Wrong Questions

ELISE KEA

outskirtspress
DENVER, COLORADO

Dedicated to my mother
Who has always believed in God's Devine Plan

Table of Contents

Lord whatever you are doing in this season, please do not do it without me.

"Don't Do It With Out Me,"

Bishop Paul S. Norton

Sometimes, we ask the
wrong questions.
Why
Not
Me?

True life story of
being diagnosed with
Lupus and Guillain-Barre
in less than a six month
time span.
By: Elise Kea

Introduction

I am a survivor. Wow, you can truly empower yourself by simply saying those four words. Try not to speak in past or future tense. Don't say "I am going to survive", or "I survived", but state the now, the present, your current state of mind. A lot of well-known authors or speakers have several degrees or magnificent documentation of an event or belief they mean to justify or explain. All I have to present is experience. Yes I am barely in my late 20's, just getting into my career, still searching for the perfect answers in life. But like with many other survivors God allowed "hell and high-water", to flood and destroy my sanctuary. Then he gave me a way out. I probably took the long way home. You know the one that you know is likely to be chaotic but you rather take that chance than be patient on a calm and peaceful road. So at first my mind is racing and I'm contemplating my beliefs and asking why me? What will I get from this? What are you doing? Through asking those questions and not thinking that I was getting a reply when I really was, I learned that sometimes He will use situations we perceive to be the most life-altering to teach us simple, basic skills. Skills like: prayer, supplication, faith, patience or long-suffering, and witnessing; witnessing and sharing being the anchor.

See I am a survivor…for a reason. Not because I deserve to be that is for certain. So anyone that is thinking that you are "still here", but has never sacrificed for another person or prayed for a stranger's soul; you are just taking up air. Survival is pulling through in spite of, and then? See that "and then"? Survival is not reached, it is continuous. After you remain you must pass on what helped you endure. That way the spirit of perseverance is passed on. We have to encourage one another. Encouragement is just one of the many qualities of a servant's heart.

The world witnessed Lauren Hill battle with brain cancer and play her first collegiate basketball game. Shannon Russell, with USA TODAY Sports wrote about Hill's desire to play for Mount St. Joseph's women's basketball team, even as she battled a brain tumor. The way I see it, she was in constant survival mode. I sat at home on Nov. 2, 2014 and marveled at how she did not stop smiling, at her firm determination to still play, and her push for the initiative of research. Shannon Russell also quoted the head basketball coach of Mount St. Joseph as saying, *"And here instead of me teaching them, it was Lauren teaching them. She's made a great impact on these young ladies. I think they're going to remember this life lesson forever and hopefully they carry it out and help her carry the mission in their own lives."* (3) She was a survivor that passed on what was going to help others endure. Your story might not help everyone, but it will touch someone. There are over 7 billion people on this planet (5). It will touch someone. Let your story be beautiful as I pray that you find beauty in mine.

1

H. I. A. B.
(Heard it all before)

I will never say those words again. As a matter of fact, only God can say those words. After being diagnosed with Lupus in late March, 2013, I realized that there were a lot of new phrases or terms I would become familiar with that I've never heard before. For instance, the term "autoimmune disease." A what? According to the U.S. National Library of Medicine, Systemic Lupus Erythematosus, also known as SLE, is an autoimmune disease in which the body's immune system mistakenly attacks the healthy tissues. It can affect the skin, joints, kidneys, brain and other organs (2). To top it off it leads to long-term chronic inflammation. I did not need a dictionary or encyclopedia to know what inflammatory meant. By looking at the swelling in my legs and hands and knowing that "chronic" means prolonged or long-term, I figured out very quickly that this would be a marathon and not a sprint. Sitting in the doctors' office, I wished I had understood the SYMPTOMS. Lord, I wish I had known half of the things that were happening to me WERE SYMPTOMS. But the words that were coming out of this tall, lean, older man's mouth, were foreign to me. I was in a hurry because I had to get back to work. All I knew was that we were doing a follow-up about a blood sample they had extracted a while back. To this day, I do not know if I should have went there alone. Some would say, "You didn't know," but I felt something was not right. This was my first encounter with this doctor. Never seen him, never met him, so I got very uncomfortable when I realized (by his mannerisms) that we were about to discuss something life altering. It felt like I got the breath knocked out of me 3 times.

"You are anemic."

"There is something different about your blood. We are going to send your samples to a specialist."

"Factors in your blood test lead me to believe you have a disease called Lupus."

No, he did not break it to me like that, but it felt like he did. It felt like a buildup of not good to bad to worse. "I know this is a lot for you to digest right now. But I want you to be aware."

There is an intense feeling of disappointment anytime you realize the difference between pain and hurt. Pain seems so much more bearable than the other. As I scheduled my next appointment at the front desk, I became overwhelmed and started crying. I walked out of that clinic a different person mentally, physically and spiritually. Mentally I was broken and confused; physically, I felt weak like Superman when he was first introduced to kryptonite; and spiritually I felt betrayed like, "Wow God, why me?"

Driving back to Nolanville all I could think about was if it was going to stop me from being able to go to the New Orleans Final Four Camp. It's a camp they host every year in the select state the women's final four basketball championship is in. I had been training for it since December. I hoped they could just give me something to make it go away like they did before.

Rewind....

Couple of weeks before, the women's league basketball team I played for called the Dominators, were to play the Dream in the semifinals. It was a Tuesday and the game was scheduled for Saturday morning at 11 AM at my favorite place to be, Lions Park Recreation Center.

The day was like any other except my hands had been swollen since I had awaken. Weird things had been happening lately but I did not pay it any mind because between work and working out, I didn't have time to pay attention to the little things. I mean I had just got the job five months ago. Got to be honest I did not think I would love it like I did. Working with kids is a time consuming responsibility, and it's something I didn't want to just hop into if I was not serious about it. At first, I thought, "Nope," working at a school will get in the way of my training. But my mother, Rosa, and my brother Tony would not let me go a day without thinking about it.

I remember when I told them I had been offered a job as an Instructional Assistant at R.E.C; "Do not be crazy," my brother implied." You do not want to miss out on a chance to affect young people's lives in a positive way."

"Yes", my mom agreed. She worked in a separate department at the school that was trying to hire me. I felt stupid for even thinking twice about it. Kids are the future. Well, I got hired in October of 2012 and somehow found time to work and play for a semi-pro team down in Austin. I enjoyed traveling with them, but that drive was tough. I started feeling exhausted at work and it just felt like too much at that time. So, the Austin trips stopped. December rolled in and I was dreading almost every second outdoors because I hated the cold. Plus at the job almost every staff member had a morning or afternoon duty. My duty was to be the adult that kindly guided kids safely across the street, also known as the "Crossing Guard."

Back to the Lupus. In December I started showing symptoms. I thought my symptoms were just problems you face from being out in the cold too much or too long. And since it was around December, I started preparing for the Final Four Camp. I really did not realize what was happening to my body. From then to March I ignored joint pain, fatigue, and memory loss, black patches on my skin, and swelling (which is inflammation). If I had a message to preach I would tell everyone DO NOT IGNORE THE SIGNS. I said to myself the joint pain must be from standing out it the cold during duty in the morning, the fatigue is from the kids and my working out twice a day, the memory loss is from fatigue, and the dark marks on my skin must be because I am not eating the right foods or drinking enough water. The swelling in my hands and my lymph nodes around my neck will surely go away. I hope anyone reading this realizes how crazy it would be to ignore any signs dealing with your health. And I had all of these symptoms all the way up to the day I got diagnosed.

But on that Thursday (the Thursday before my semifinals game with the Dominators), I did not know what the swelling meant. I went to some coworkers and asked questions but the most I got was "Yeah you need to get that checked out." Basically it looked like I had tiny knots on my neck and under my ears. So I decided to go to the urgent care clinic on a Friday. Sad thing about it is I just wanted them to make the swelling go away so that I could play the next day. The physician had no answer about my hands, but told me my lymph node situation was likely because of something going on in my immune system, hint, hint.

"I can give you a quick injection that can clear those lumps right up, "the physician said. "And I will send you home with some anti-inflammatory pills and hopefully that will bring down the swelling. If that does not work after a couple of days them stop taking it." Sounded pretty easy to me. He shook my hand and exited as the nurse came in to give me the injection in my...... "In your rear." She insisted, "It goes through your system faster when we inject you there." At least she was not mean looking. And if she was what could I do? Rhetorical. Oh my goodness. Oh my goodness. I was already afraid of needles. Now she was telling me I had to get it basically in my tush?

I remember when I was in middle school, I make it known to my family I wanted to make it to the WNBA. I do not recall who it was to be exactly, but they said, "You have to be tough to make it there Lise (my name for short). You're afraid of shots and at the professional level when you get physicals they give you shots in your butt." And yes this conversation really happened.

All I remember is I said, "Well I guess I'm not going to the WNBA." Shame right. It's a good thing that I was 23 years old that time around. Then again, 2 years prior, I probably would have ran out of that clinic basketball shorts hanging off me and all. But I really wanted to play in the semifinals game without anything hurting. It was quick and painless. It's crazy how you can mentally torture yourself to believe something is worse than it actually is.

When I got home of course my mom was concerned. She had been watching my body do some, like I explained, very weird things lately. I told her the physician had no answer and that he gave me some quick fixes. That night I prayed as hard as I could while taking those anti-inflammatory pills. Why did I want to play so bad? In women's league basketball, some people took it seriously and some didn't. A couple of the teams were from the outlying areas like Cove and Austin. I hadn't been playing pleasantly and the more fatigued I got, the more my body would reject itself, the more I felt like I had to prove myself. You know prove what every hooper (basketball player) tries to prove when they are done with college ball and aren't overseas; that it's not over for them! That there's still a chance. I just knew we were going to win against a team we were 0-2 against during regular season.

I woke up and raced to the bathroom. What in the world! My hands were the skinniest I had seen in a while. Those pills were magic! My joints and my fingers were still sore but it was very bearable. Yep, yep, it was GAME TIME! I went to Lions Park a little earlier than game time. We were going to be missing both of our main big girls, so I had to be ready to bring it. I shot for about 45 minutes straight. Oh yea buckets...swisssh... baseline jumper...cash! They say if you are at the gym by yourself, then the best sweat you can get is by playing yourself one-on-one, like in *Above The Rim*.

We trailed most of the game but victory still seemed close. I thought I played well that game, but my grandmother told me I was falling all over the place. She has always been my biggest fan. In middle school when I played at Manor, she just clapped. But in high school, I wasn't so lucky. After the games, if I didn't show out she asked questions. "Why were you so passive? Or you didn't play your game tonight sweetie," she would say. But I must say she was usually accurate, and during the game, she was always positive.

Through the years, she started to understand the game more. I would hear her in the stands sometimes telling my mom what was a foul and what was not. My grandmother was best known for her phrase, "Let's go ladies" and "Girls gone wild." Especially if the other team was fouling my squad, she'd say, "Oh boy those girls gone wild." It would always give the crowd a laugh, but that day with all her cheering and our great effort we still came up short. Yes, we lost to a team from Austin. Dang! But I had to stay in shape for Final Four Camp. So back to playing at KPR with the guys till then. These are just some of the events that happened to me in March of 2013.

Take a Moment: *What if God after blessing you and blessing you allowed you to endure pain that could potentially last a lifetime? Then He said, "Don't curse me and die, but continue to bless other people." Could you do it? What steps would you take?*

2

Final Four Camp

It had been almost 3 weeks since I sat in the clinic, and the doctor told me he suspected I had "Lupus." He was now my primary care doctor. I didn't have one before then, but after we shared that personal moment, I didn't want anyone else. Thing is, after I left there that day, I tried to go about life as normally as possible. Yes, I told my mother about what was going on, but I did not let my family or friends know for another month and-a-half; some later than others for certain reasons.

Initially I told my mother that the appointment went well, but after constant runs to the pharmacy I had to tell her something. "I have Lupus mom. I did not know how to tell you so I've just been waiting." She sat in the car and stared at me searching for strength out of the window. "God has the last say sweetie." That is so true, I thought. But what if I don't agree with his last say?

I just wanted to concentrate on the camp, and I guess I tried to make myself believe that when I got back from New Orleans the lab results and bloodwork would say something totally different. Maybe if I had faith like the man with leprosy in Matthew, Chapter 8, it would have happened that way. But God is a God of his OWN explanations. I've learned not to question Him….as much.

I was sure glad I bought my plane ticket ahead of time and got my personal days approved by my boss. I would leave Wednesday, April 3rd and be back after the last evaluation game on Saturday, April 6th. This would be a testy weekend for my mom and me since she would be babysitting our new puppy Maxine. My mom loves me dearly, but she was not much of a dog lover at this point in time. We joked about me having to pay her for each day and I probably should have. I would have been driving to New Orleans if I was not going alone. My Mazda was surely good on gas and mileage, but nine hours was too far for me to drive. So my new car caught some dust at home. It was my 2012 Christmas gift to myself.

It was only an hour and a half flight from Dallas to New Orleans. As I got off of the plane, I felt excited, nervous, heavy-hearted, honored, all those things. Thank God the hotel was right across the street from the airport. I took the shuttle over and got ready to check in with one thing on my mind, "A hot shower." The reservation manager at the front desk couldn't find my name under April 3rd. I was in panic mode thinking that I was going to have to pull a *Pursuit of Happiness* in the restroom. How could I have booked the hotel for the 4th through the 5th and not have realized it.

As I always traveled, I went with just enough, so when she suggested I pay the $130 for the night, I just stared at her for a second then called my mom. I knew she was about to dig her daughter out of this funk. I guess I thought she was a magician. A stranger walked past me and then for some reason, WINK WINK (GOD), she turned around and asked me if I needed a room and that she would not mind sharing. Her name was Linda. I remember because I got it wrong for the first two days. Great thing about it is she happened to know two other players that drove in from Kentucky so we had a ride wherever we wanted to go. So glad that I had a place to lay my head that night, but the next day was a big day either way.

DAY 1

Linda and I got up early next morning to eat at the IHOP across the street. The two Kentucky girls met with us and we ate like there was no tomorrow. One of the Kentucky girl's name was Jade. I only remember because she turned out to be an assassin on the court. No taller than 5' but could pat the rock (great ball handling) and shoot. She was a good point guard no doubt. After we ate, I rode with the ladies to Walmart to pick up some snacks and food just in case I got hungry in the middle of the night. Got back and had to rush to put my things up in my room because registration had begun.

Basically, we waited in line, got our jerseys and made sure everything was correct in our player bio. It was held inside a small conference room on the 1st floor of the hotel. Practice was hours later. There would be two practices. Which one you participated in depended on what team you had been placed on. Found out I had to practice first but half our players weren't checked in yet so we had to go ahead with the 11 we had. We warmed up with a couple of laps around the upper floor of the gymnasium then we got to business.

The team coaches had good sense of humor, good manners. They were just the go-get-it type. One of them was tall and light-skinned; he kept looking at me waiting for me to break out of my shell. But I was exhausted and a bit timid. We practiced like we didn't have a game the next day. But I had a good feeling about things. As our practice concluded about 100 girls were in the stands and arriving. Maybe not, but whatever the number was it rounded up to one double zero. I remember wishing I was in that group so that I would not be so tired. Amongst those were people that were supposed to be at our practice but just happened to arrive late.

In the crowd I also saw an old teammate from my Texas College days, British Thomas. I knew she was coming. We had communicated via Twitter. She was an All-American and me, Honorable Mention 2nd Team All-Conference. So we represented Texas College well. She graduated a year before me, Elise Kea, Bachelor of Science in Physical Education. And I wasn't using my degree that's why I was trying to get an overseas contact. Though I did enjoy my job and my co-workers, my love was and is basketball.

I walked over to Brit after practice to say what's up. It was nice to see a familiar face. She told me I had gotten skinnier. That was funny to me because in college I stayed in the weight room. I wanted to stay and watch the other teams practice, but I was so tired and hungry at that. Plus we had combine testing the next day and games. I wish I would have stayed though because it rumored the next day that the overseas players were showing out. I wish I had participated in more activities in New Orleans. Sometimes you can get so caught up in experiencing the moment you don't even enjoy it as much as you should.

DIARY NOTES:
4/5/13

Yesterday we had practice and today we did combine testing and played games.

I am exhausted. I have never been so tired in all my life.

I am thankful for this experience.

Some of these girls are really good.

I need to get in better shape.

We played at 11:45 and now I got moved to the Iceland team. We play at 2:15. God give me the strength to power through. My body is shut down. Well about to rest. I'm in New Orleans, Louisiana at the Final 4 Combine.

DAY 2

All the point guards, guards and post split up for the first part of the day. We had to complete something that to me was the hardest part of camp; a 3-minute video workout. And it was not all that hard, but exhausting. "Three minutes!" I'm sure everybody was laughing at the thought. But after, everyone was just glad it was over. To complete our personal Hello, I'm Elise Kea and this is what I can do video, we each needed a partner. Did not have to look much farther. There was British. The training coach asked who wanted to go first and everyone looked around, so Brit and I ran out first. Since I would go first, she would be my rebounder, private cheer-squad, you know confidant. And then I for her. During the video workout, I heard a guard on the side say it sounded like I had asthma. Ha, ha, Ha, Ha, Ha. It was funny then and it's funnier now. I only made a couple of jumpers but I made a lot of 3's like in college. When it was time to switch Brit did her mid-range and floaters just like in college.

After we were done, it was time for combine testing. Easy Peezy. I was amazed at the athletes that were there. They had to raise the pole at the vertical station for some girls that were there. After testing, we got a good hour of rest at the gym, then evaluation games started. I can't recall if I played one or two games that day, but I sure remember the first one. It was a close game, but I did not do my part to help my team win. There was a girl guarding me, slightly hand checking, and it felt like I couldn't go by her. It was like I had bricks in my shoes. I was just out there in the way. But through it all, you got to keep your head high and give your all. I did. After each game that weekend, I kept asking myself if I should have waited and trained more. But physicality is only one aspect of the game. My mental was not right. Words to the wise: When you realize you are not the fastest, strongest and toughest, you better be the bravest. You better believe.

Again there were activities after we were done on the court but I was wiped out. Who knows who I would have me if I would have went to Bourbon Street. And I am star struck easily, so I would have loved to have met the couple of WNBA players that I heard were there via Twitter. But after the game, I rode with the Kentucky girls to Popeye's and then crashed in my room. I mean literally crashed. Definition – food in bed, TV on, one sock on, mouth open. A good rest for my last day at camp. My plane would fly out shortly after my last game.

DAY 3

I remember waking up and feeling like I needed a couple ice-baths. Sore and all, though I was ready to play. I honestly had amnesia of the previous game. That's how you have to be in life sometimes. My team was up first today. I played better but not exactly how I would've hoped. I was definitely looser and not as dull. I hit a three and made a little reverse lay-up. Guess I had just a little more confidence period, but I still got out shined by girls that were executing at the highest possible level. After the game I kicked back on a wall in the corner of the gym and ate my subway a player had brought to me. I had eaten with her father and friend that happened to be on my team the night before.

Oh that's right. When I had gotten back to my room the night before I did not enjoy the chicken so much. I was expecting it to be "Outstanding" because it was Popeye's and we were in Louisiana, but it just didn't hit the spot for me. The Popeye's in Killeen tastes better. Sooooo because of this, I went down to the IHOP beside the hotel and ordered a salad. While I waited I sat and conversed with them (the girl, her father, her friend). She was about 6' 2' and she had a soft voice you would never expect. I wanted to nickname her Tree or Lanky. When my salad came, I bid them a goodnight. Then I went to my room and crashed. Same definition.

As I ate my subway the next game started. I was hype because I had seen a girl in warm-ups (pre-game shooting) that reminded me of me. She was humble but confident. She was buffer, faster and bigger than me though. (I really did not like writing that). Some players only care about themselves, but I get excited about other good players as well. I'll tell anybody that game was so intense it was like it was on ESPN. Back and forth. Back and forth. Then the lead got stretched out at the end. I was sweating watching. Jade did her thing and the bigger me did her thing. That means they played good.

The gym started to get packed with parents and scouts. All players know a scout when they see one. They come in with the one strap book bag, collar shirt tucked in or fitted cap. Or they walk in like they can take everybody in the gym to the hoop. Yep I know a scout when I see one and they were coming in left and right along with players' college coaches that were there to support them. British and I went to camp in 2011 when we were seniors on the court; our coaches went with us then.

The final four Camp Coaches announced there would be one last game. Players they selected would be added on to the two teams that just played. That would be the championship. Tree got picked, Linda got picked and Brit got picked. I did not. Yea it hurt but I still cheered them on. Linda had that lock down defense. And British was aggressive, fearless as always. She made a lot of baskets. It was a good game to watch. As it was ending and I finally was taking my basketball shoes off, one of the coaches asked me if I wanted to play another game.

The gym was emptying out and the cameras were being put away. What would I say? "Sure," I replied while putting my shoes back on. My new basketball shoes I had bought just for the camp. Shoes that were a little too clean for me. Time to scuff'em up some more doing what I love. No crowd, but some little feeling deep inside that I'm playing for something else. So I laced up and got on the court. He combined all the players that did not play the last game and some that did into one massive group and told us to line up along the baseline. When we did the coaches picked who they wanted on the two teams. I was the third to last pick. When I think about it was enough to suck the life out someone. But out of all the games, I can say I played well in that one. Made a couple baskets, got some assists, and steals. We almost busted the clock (reached 100 points on the scoreboard). "Way to finish the race, Elise," I thought. It's not over till it's over. We said our goodbyes to the coaches and waited for the shuttle to take us back to the hotel.

My checkout time had already passed so I took my things to Linda's room so I could shower before my flight. "I saw you today," she said. "You were way more confident." I appreciated it, but I was sad the experience was almost over. Nice people. Nice weekend. Time to go home. At the airport I saw another girl that had a rough weekend like me. I told her to keep doing her thing.

Take a Moment: *Why are we so stiff when we shoot for the stars? When we are chasing our dreams, all we care about is that dream. In almost every sermon that prophetess Juanita Bynum has preached, she talks about "the process." It's not about just being saved, but it is about making mistakes, learning, striving and elevating yourself. I should have enjoyed the process of that camp. The meeting new people, the beautiful places, and learning from other players.*

3

Lupus

Ever watched Diary of a Wimpy Kid? Well there is a part in the movie where the older brother is trying to teach the little brother some of the secrets to an easy life. He told him to lower his parents' expectations, by telling them he probably would fail math. So that when he came home with an average grade they would be satisfied. Crazy, right? But I should have considered that trick regarding the camp. I was so excited and pumped about it, that I raved to all my co-workers, my boss, and those sweet kids about how important it was. I told them about my training and how I worked out twice a day. Oh boy! I know their expectations were high because my expectations were high. So to come back to work with average news was a letdown. I did not say a word. I emailed it out. I told my coworkers that I did not make the overseas team, but that I enjoyed the experience.

Explaining to adults is easy, but explaining to kids is hard. "Why didn't you make it? Did you do good? Did you do bad?" And adults are easily let down, but kids ... kids make you feel bad. After a couple of weeks the questions dyed down, but

I couldn't stop thinking about it. I mean it felt like I totally fumbled. It was not a bad situation to be in though. Coming back to a job I enjoyed and kids saying they were glad I was not going anywhere. Lucky me. And I'm still going to go and hoop with the guys because you never know. You should always be ready. Weeks passed and it was already time to go see the rheumatologist (they specialize in dealing with clinical problems involving joints, soft tissues, autoimmune diseases, and other disorders).

My primary care doctor had made the appointment shortly before I left for camp. He told me that he was not 100% sure but that he suspected it was Systemic Lupus. I held on to that uncertainty, even if it was only 1% of it. But this rheumatology specialist had the definite answer. The clinic had sent my bloodwork over and they would analyze it. In walked a nice looking young man. He examined me and told me after the examination he would elaborate on what he was looking for and what it might tell him. But he had some questions of his own. So he brought in the M.D.

I figured she was the head lady. She cited signs of inflammation in my knees and legs. And parts of me that were supposed to be firm were squishy. "O.K.! let's see here." She pulled out my blood work and explained some things to me, but I was zoned out because I had not heard the word Lupus yet. "So do I have Lupus?" my eyes widened. "Yes, yes, you do." Deep inside I knew it so I dared not cry again. "What is important now is making sure it has not affected any vital organs." So I had to get more bloodwork and a urine sample.

I needed time to clear my head so I hoped that it took a couple of days for the lab results. Wishful thinking. I was over my brother Tony's house chatting with my sister-in-law when the rheumatologist called. I took a deep breath then walked to a quiet corner by the front door. The Lupus had reached my kidneys and they were leaking protein. I broke down in tears and probably startled my caller. Several months later she told me she would have never known how tough I was through that phone call. So what's next? How do we start beating this? I would have to go to a kidney doctor for more details on what steps to take.

My rheumatologist, Dr. C, wasted no time scheduling me an appointment. I would see the kidney specialist in a couple of weeks.

My father was in town and offered to go with me to my appointment. It was June and school was out so there was time to enjoy him. Dr. G., my kidney doctor, confirmed my leaking of protein and guided me through the steps we would take to recover and improve. On June 19th, I would be scheduled for a kidney biopsy. That was not too far away. Oh boy, I was super nervous and jittery.

Father's Day had come. I bought my dad a card and added my own flavor to it with pictures of my two brothers and me in it. I also bought him some peanuts. It's a country thing. He accepted both gifts with a smile. The previous day I took him to a pool bar. He did not know I could "get down" with a pool stick. He kept complimenting me. I told him, "Come on dad I'm an athlete." He had an old school game like Shaft or something. "Who's that man with a master plan? Daddy! He is a bad shut yo mouth."

We had a good time but had to leave because of all that smoking at the bar. He enjoyed his stay but had to go back to N.C. for his own appointment. He made sure we chomped down on some good Chinese food before he left though, at a buffet with all-you-can-eat crab legs.

June 19th came faster than customers when the new iPhone

comes out. It felt like I blinked twice and it was there. After the procedure, I would stay in the hospital overnight just for precautionary reasons. My mother and grandmother escorted me there. My aunt who works at the hospital peaked her head in and chatted with us. When the nurse called my name, I got so nervous she noticed me shaking. She was going to talk me through the process so I could relax and not worry too much. My aunt kept telling me it wouldn't be that bad but I was not listening.

It took a couple of minutes for me to relax my head on the pillow. I was positioned on my stomach and they say the worst thing during the procedure is hearing the doctors' talk about you or what they are doing to you. I was glad Dr. G. was conducting my biopsy because she was cool and laid back. For some reason I trusted her real early. "All done." The procedure was over and I got to flip back over to my back. Restrictions: No getting up for 8 hours. Now that's a long time to be awake and on your back. While waiting for a room they brought me a nice hot hospital meal. It was not easy eating at a 135 degree angle, but I did it.

Staying overnight was very tough for me. First of all, I'm the baby. I don't like to be called the baby but I am. So I guess I expected to be checked on every second of the night because the next day I was pouting. I told my mom I was lonely. I guess it was kind of my fault. My grandmother asked me if I wanted her to stay but I said that I was fine. Trying to be a tough 24 year old. My aunt kept reminding me that she thought I was spoiled. I denied the truth, "nuh uh."

It had been a rough night. Not a bad one just a grind out type of night. Both my brothers and my dad checked on me, but after that it's like time stood still. I could not sleep and my back was sore. You find out who you are in your time alone. Do you choose to fret? Maybe reminisce. Think of all the negative things going on in your life. Or maybe talk to God. I did all four, but I mostly talked to God. Soon he would reply and make me pay close attention.

My mother, grandmother, aunt and I were all sharing laughs in my hospital room when the doctors arrived. Dr. G had to be somewhere else so she sent a replacement. I looked at him funny. I could not help it. I did not know him and he was delivering serious information. I had something called Lupus Nephritis in my kidneys. They assured me it was at a less severe Stage 5 and could be controlled. Then came the list of medications: Prednisone, Tramadol, Gabapentin, and some unknown brand. I had to have a word. "Why do I need this one?" Their tone suddenly turned bossy.

4

Our Little Secret

My mom was the first to know about my Lupus. Then I believe I told my Dad, my brothers, my aunt and lastly my grandmother because I knew she would worry the most. Nobody knew my struggles like my mom did because she got to see them up close every day. It became something we just kept to ourselves.

Work began to get more difficult in the days after I came back from camp. But it was not fatigue that was kicking my butt the most; it was the onset of neuropathy, which is nerve damage. Too bad I caught on late. All I knew was that my feet would go numb and then tingle. I figured I needed more comfortable shoes. I also started suffering "heat attacks", in which my body would feel like it was burning up. My grandma would joke that our house was an ice chest but it was only because I kept bothering mom that it was too hot in it.

At my job I worked in one particular classroom the most, but I also peaked in and helped with the other 1st grade level classrooms as well. In my main room, I wondered if my weakness was becoming apparent. I used to stand more and interact more. I found myself sitting down when I should have been standing. Especially in physical activities my body just would not last. The kids were used to me running with them around the gym when they did laps. We would race and I loved the smiles on their faces when I would let them win. I repeat, "Let them win." But I could not do that anymore. I'd play dodgeball and other games, which left me exhausted at the end of the day. It was obvious to me I was not the long-lasting energizer bunny anymore.

At the beginning of the school year I had cross-guard duty in the morning. It was a little hard to make it on time everyday so a staff member was kind enough to offer to switch times with me. She would take my morning duty and I would take her afternoon one. About a week later I had an appointment with my rheumatologist and her biggest advice to me was "Stay out of the sun." Great! How was I going to pull this off? She informed me that sunlight triggers Lupus flare ups. A flare up could be my joints aching or a "heat attack," maybe a head-ache, upset stomach, or even swelling. When I told my mom, she just advised me to keep an umbrella in my car and take it out at the end of the day when it's time for duty. Smart lady.

Field day was not too far away and I was stressing about it. I really wanted to participate but I had not been feeling so well lately. It did not take much to change my mind about sitting out. My main teacher offering to buy me a field day t-shirt was the first straw. Seeing the set-up and all the fun stations was the second. There was no way I was going to miss Field Day.

By this time I had informed the main teacher that I worked with of my situation. It would have been unfair to not let her know why I was missing so many half-days for doctor appoint-ments. She was nothing but understanding and always asked how I was doing.

Field Day was a blast. I know you are wondering how I made it all day in the sun. I borrowed some sunscreen from a co-worker and prayed I would not sweat it off. All was well and all went well. With the school year coming to a close, all I could think was "I made it." In reality I had a long way to go. At the end of the school year you have to get all your paperwork together to turn into your supervisor and also pack up your classroom. Plus my mother and I were moving from a house to an apartment. It was nearby, thank the Lord.

In the last week of school it was like an unfriendly giant had awoken. My joints were hurting so badly and the headaches would not cease. The numbness and tingling in my feet turned to burning and would not go away. At the end of the day I had to sit down and rest my limbs. In one instance I had to go to my boss and ask if I could be excused. There were only thirty-minutes until the bell would ring, but I could not last that long and have duty at the end of the day. I broke down out of nowhere. He asked me to close his office door. "Are you alright? Tell me what's going on." "I have Lupus."

"O.K., are you having a flare-up?" I nodded. He told me to go ahead and go home and that his assistant would take care of checking me out. I guess he knew about it a little because he handled it so professionally. I rushed home and prayed while I was driving because my headache barely let me see the road. When I made it to the somewhat empty house, I hopped on the couch and didn't move till morning. Harder days would come.

It was the last day of school for the faculty and staff. The kids had been let go the previous day and we were slowly closing the page on the 2012-2013 school year. I tried to help out any way I could anywhere I could. A lot of teachers were almost done packing and storing up their stuff. It my main room it was kind of a different story. She was changing rooms so she had to pack up and move everything. My heart was willing but my body was not. She was working so hard to get it done and said she probably would be there till evening.

I planned on staying with her. I packed and packed but it appeared I had not even dented the mass. There was so much left. I had to rest and take a break. I went to my mom's room upstairs and laid down on the floor with a pillow she had. Only reason we could work at the same place is because she worked in a different program. They called me little Kea even though I was the tall one. Mom sits at about 5'3." I give myself an extra inch when I say 5"8."

After a good 15-minute nap it was time to return to help in my main room. By that time another dent was put into the mass. My head was now throbbing and all I could do was count down till the last minutes of the work day. I hated to leave her but I had too. I could not feel my legs under me. All I felt was sharp pain striking like lightning through all of my limbs. That night I wished I could go back in time to help move because I really liked that teacher. I liked all my teachers, but in my assigned room I felt it was a commitment and trust I needed to uphold. Which I felt I did not. I could not! I was too tired and in too much pain. The spirit is willing but the flesh is weak (Matthew 26:41). Darn, I hated leaving her to do all that work at the school. Bus she was a tough one.

When my dad came down in June the neuropathy pain had

reached new heights. I did not like standing for long periods of time because my legs felt like boulders. I remember distinctively telling my mom that we may have to get them cut off. "Stop talking like that Elise." But it was the way I felt. One day my dad and I went to visit an old church friend in the hospital. We enjoyed entertaining this sweet lady but the enjoyment was short-lived. When my fatigue kicked in, it was like living was exhausting. I suddenly became tired just sitting there in that hospital chair. Talking was tiring, laughing was tiring.

In came two more visitors. One seemingly smelled of smoke. My dad's eyes caught mines. We nodded and agreed, time to go! And why is my heart racing so fast? We said our see you laters and split. Stomach growling and head hurting. I had a taste for chicken. We stopped at Popeye's (way better that the one I had in New Orleans) and got some quick lunch boxes to go. Shrimp and fries, yum, yum. Yes I know I said I had a taste for chicken, but daddy came out with shrimp. I was fine with it. Yum, yum.

For some time I had been going to my grandmother's house for soothing purposes. Though it was usually always freezing at our apartment, I just could not get a good feeling of the cold air. I needed an old fashioned AC unit to blow directly on me because I was burning up all over.

These new meds had me feeling all types of ways – headaches, fever, mood swings. But for that past week, if I could just make it to my grandma's house I felt O.K. I would lie down on leather couch. It would cool my skin. She would get me a blanket and turn the AC unit on (it was by the front door – blows right on the couch) and I would not move for hours and hours. My mom became concerned.

We had just moved into the apartments, so I know the fact that I never wanted to be there lately made her worry. She asked me to come home on occasions and I would tell her that I couldn't for a while. I explained that it was like grandma's house was spiritually covered in some type of way because as soon as I would lie down on that couch I had relief.

So after my dad and I got our Popeye's I asked him to take me to my grandmas. My feet were on fire and I was almost in tears. I laid on that couch for hours, covers over my whole body except for my feet. Anything that touched my toes would send a burning sensation down the nerves in my feet. This was too painful and I did not know what to do so I called my aunt who is in the medical field. All night we tried to find answers. I told her my neuropathy symptoms and triggers. She started searching Lupus forums and websites.

Wow, I didn't know all these people had Lupus as well. Some were going through exactly what I was, at a later age maybe a different pace. "Found it!" she began reading. "Lately I have been experiencing chronic pain and burning sensation in my feet. It hurts to stand, it hurts to…." she went on. The lady on the forum basically explained and confirmed that she had to go to a neurologist about the nerve pain in her feet. My aunt told me to not wait till it got too much worse. Again it was time to go see a doctor. The Lupus forum really helped me in understanding that there would be a lot more experiences to come but that I could help prevent some and that I was not alone.

Well the atmosphere of grandma's home did its job again. I felt better. It was late and I didn't feel like getting up but I knew I couldn't sleep comfortably through the night on the couch. I needed a bed so I went home. Both parents slept as I laid awake in my bed. Awake all night. What in the world?

Was I not sleeping because my heart was racing so fast? I didn't know what that was all about but I knew it wasn't normal. The next day I woke up in pain. From when I opened my eyes after maybe an hour's sleep I could feel fire racing through each and every toe. I wasted no time that day. My mind was set on pain relief. As my mom lay asleep I got dressed and rushed to the nearest urgent care clinic. I was there extra early. The doors had not even opened yet. When the doors finally opened I rushed inside. I needed help immediately. How could I tell? My heart was dang near beating out of my chest. When the nurse checked my beats per minute, I was at 145. He asked me if I was O.K. "Yes, I feel fine. My feet just burn really, really bad."

The urgent care doctor wanted to draw some blood. She said it was obvious something was going on. She said I needed fluids bad. Why did I have to be a hard stick? Got stuck 3 times. IV wouldn't go in my arm. Another nurse had to come in and try. Finally! That was a little painful. I ranted about my nerve pain in my feet, and I told her I didn't think I could go another day without medication for it. I left the clinic with meds for my neuropathy and for my heartbeat. Only words that haunted me were, "Those pills won't work right away." She said it was going to take up to a week for it to take effect. Oh boy hope I can last that long.

Take A Moment: *Why do we ask for temporary healing? Or we look for the earthly answer first before consulting God. We prolong things so much. We prolong the process. But it is okay, we are human and will learn by examining others' mistakes.*

5

"Open Gym"

As much pain as it felt like I was in, nothing was going to stop me from playing ball. I wish I could have been playing on a semi-pro team, but since I wasn't, open gym was my time to do what I love. Didn't really care for the beaches or lakes. I'm a family girl. They are my friends, movie buddies, kick-it partners, etc. I'm a loner for the most part. Been like that all of my life I think. I'm like Joshua Sloccum the ultimate loner. Sailed across the world in his ship. He was soul searching to me. It took him 3 years on water. Anyways my membership had expired at the local gym so other than working out in my apartments weight room, open-gym was my other outlet.

My old high school opened the gum often because a lot of girls wanted to play and get a good workout in. For the most part of June, I'd sleep, grimace in pain and then go play ball. In my head the pain was temporary. I just knew that it would go away. KHS was where I graduated high school. Appreciate everything I learned there. I feel like it's a monument because it is named after my city...good old Killeen. Have a pretty good relationship with the coach of the basketball team. When I went off to college, she came to a couple games nearby and stayed updated on how I was doing. I remember I got to go overseas to play with USAAI in Greece and Italy in 2010 and she gave me a considerable donation to help with my travels. Our relationship was genuine. We both loved basketball.

At the first open gym everyone was there. Graduates from all the local schools came home from college. I was a little older than some but it was fun. And it was packed so if you lost you were off the court till the next open gym basically.

I hadn't really opened up to anybody about what was going on with my body except my mom. My team had lost and I sat down next to coach to catch up on old times. My freshman year I played on the freshman team and we were "cold" (really good.) Then my sophomore year, I was on JV and got moved to Varsity. Oh yea bright lights! But I failed off the team and didn't realize my impact till I couldn't play. When I came back, she made sure I stayed on JV so I could learn my lesson. Junior year I was a changed girl. Failing is not cool. Senior year 2007, she awarded me MVP. I was surprised but she believed in me.

I looked at her and smiled "What's up coach?" "Nothing much how have you been doing?" She continued watching the girls play. I felt a little ashamed about my Lupus. I mean I at least for some time was a sort of role model for younger players. At least I hope I was. That person she could speak on and say, "Yes Elise Kea, she played here and she worked hard. She's doing good trying to go overseas." How do I tell her I'm not the same anymore? I started out calm, "Coach I need to tell you something." She turned her attention away from the game and looked at me concerned. "In late March early April, I was diagnosed with Lupus." I felt like I caught her off guard, her face was so stunned. I started to break down. "Coach I'll never be the same again. I'm not going to be able to play ball anymore." She comforted me and told me yes I would still be that person. She agreed with me that it was messed up that is was happening to me, but that I could conquer it.

I needed that talk. I had been holding in those negative thoughts for so long. I needed to trust in God but since things so bad my faith decreased. Why is it that when trials come, we think it's beyond God's power when really He is letting it happen to increase our faith or others'. The next week there was not that many people there but enough to run full-court games. I was past my sulking stage. I just wanted to play ball.

As the weeks went by I got slower and slower. It's known that I'm not the fastest guard anyways, but jeez this was ridiculous. Seemingly no one noticed but me. My legs felt like stone. And not only were my feet burning, but all my shoes felt too small. I was moving so sluggish on the court, but it felt great just to be there. We won a couple of games. When you are down it feels so boss just to triumph in anything. But as weeks went by my body became less mobile.

I will never forget this particular day because it was the last time I ran up and down a basketball court in 2013. Some young buck was giving me the blues. She was driving on me, she was shooting 3's on me. I had to grab her shirt occasionally. She was blowing by me so fast. We lost but since it wasn't a bunch of people there my team was going to play again. I waved my hand and declined. "Elise, you done?" I nodded then and took off my shoes. I kind of felt like that moment was symbolic. I watched them play for a few more minutes then exited the gym. I doubted I could make it up and down the court anymore.

My birthday was fast approaching. My mom knew I was feeling down so she tried her best to get something together. She figured I wanted to be low key, so 5 would be lovely 10 was a crowd. And I believe exactly 9 people came. My mom set up nachos and wings and all the attendees did a happy birthday speech on a video on her phone. We ate, laughed and watched *Martin* all night. I tried my best to hide my pain. My feet were really burning. Goodness, why hadn't those pills kicked in yet? But the laughter overpowered my sadness after a while. I stopped thinking about basketball and Lupus and I just laughed all night.

My brother Carlos was there along with my sister-in-law and my nieces Mya and Denasia, nephew Kyre. My dad had a good time and so did some family friends. They didn't understand how much I needed them and appreciated them. I didn't sleep that night, as usual. I could tell something was about to happen. I just didn't know what to expect.

A friend of the family, who also was my grandmother's beautician, was led to hold bible study at her beauty shop on Fridays over the summer. She wanted me to speak a message from the heart to the kids that came out on June 28th. In my mind I kept refusing. "God, I am not in the mood." You know how we get when we are going through; everything has to stop because we are suffering. Our work for the kingdom has to stop, and so does our praise and worship. World stop moving because this trial is bigger than me. Bigger than Him; bigger than Him? Exactly, snap out of it! And I quickly did that because "Lise love the kids." Trials come to bring you closer to

God, not turn you away from him.

What would I talk about? I pondered and pondered and finally was led to Daniel 3: 1-30 and I began dissecting His word through my understanding. I was extremely nervous, so I kept studying so that I would feel comfortable.

When Friday came I felt horrible. I thought about cancelling but knew it would look bad. I also thought about how I attempted to get back on the court with a hip contusion in college. We go hard in the paint for the world, but get all timid for God. That continued running through my mind. So I got up and got dressed and prayed.

On the way there I started getting really hot. When people were watching I did not like for my mom to help me, but when they weren't I begged her too. I'm sure I had her all types of confused. Upon arrival, I got a feeling of approval from God. You know like he gives you a head nod that only you can see, that means "I am pleased."

After being introduced by Ms. Lucky, the jitters went away. I enjoyed and was inspired by the message. I referred back to my notes.

Daniel 3:1-30

Shadrach, Meshach, and Abed-nego are cast into a fiery furnace.
LET YOUR LIFE BRING OTHERS TO CHRIST
Have you ever been through something like a hardship or a rough time, and the way you handled it made someone (maybe a friend, family, unknown bystander) say wow who do you serve? How do I get some of that?
(Read Story)
V1-6- Ever been told what to do?
V7- And everyone does it because they are scared not to do it?
V8-12- See when you are different you stand out. You might not

think so, but when you are not doing what everyone else is doing, you stand out.
V13-18- It's not enough to be in that crowd. Sometimes you have to speak up for Jesus.

<u>*Key Points*</u>

-When you are going through or not going through, somebody is watching you.
-Being the only one does not mean you have to be a lonely one.
-Hold yourself accountable...for what? For the souls you can touch.

The young people seemed to be tuned in to what God gave me to give to them. Like I said, I spoke through my understanding. I spoke something that touched on my situation. I spoke to these children and adults approximately 1 week before a special sequencing of events. As I look back I marvel at God's artistic touch. But I will admit that it is hard to let your life be his masterpiece. After a closing prayer my grandmothers spiritual daughter Ms. Barbara surprised me with cupcakes and everyone sung happy birthday. I was totally caught off guard but I appreciated it and realized the pain was worth meeting those kids.

6

The Fall

It was the fourth of July and I felt like a hot mess. But I really wanted to do something to clear my head. I got up out of bed and got my medications together. I hated my meds routine. They were so spread out, it was easy to forget them. Lately, my grandma had been spending the night just to spend more time with us. We had one of the most comfortable couches so when I walked in the living room, she was sound asleep.

My legs were a little shaky and I had a slight headache. It was a usual thing at least that's what it seemed like. I thought to myself, "Am I going to feel like this the rest of my life?"

My mom is the breakfast Queen. She loves fixing eggs, sausage, toast and pancakes in the morning. When my grandma woke up, she was ready to eat just like me. We spoke blessings over our food, and enjoyed the hot meal. I didn't eat much. I was surely hungry but when I sat in front of the food it's like my stomach shrunk. The food was delicious, I just couldn't eat it all. I had forgotten one of my meds in the room and I was on my way to get it, slowly but surely. My mom's voice etched in the background. She was fussing at me for not eating all of my food. It wasn't the first time I didn't eat much and wouldn't be the last.

I was dramatically losing weight. Every time I went to the doctor, I dropped about 4 lbs. down. I started at 150 and now I was 132. And with the loss of weight was loss of strength. Days prior my grandma had to help me walk to the car because my legs were acting like they were going to give out. When I was on my way to get my medication, I turned the corner by my room and with my next step it felt like my legs disappeared. I could not feel anything beneath me. There I went, a slow, long, tumbling fall to the ground. And it was loud, it made a "plop" sound. I have never saw my mom or grandma move as fast as they did that day. They came running. My grandma usually used a cane but when I looked up she was looking down on me without one. I guess she had developed super-senior-citizen-powers for a moment. They helped me stand back up.

From that moment on I was treated like the baby of the family I was. I could not make a move without hearing, "Where are you going? What are you doing? You better slow down. Have you taken your medicine? You need to eat something?"

I had a severe headache that day so I predicted any 4th of July activities were going to be out of the question. Through the day I had to be escorted through my own apartment. It felt like I was walking on toothpicks. I had to grab onto things as leverage or use the shoulder of my grandma. My aunt lived in another town. My oldest brother had just recently moved, and my other brother was taking his family out for the day. The three of us were debating what we were going to do. I felt like a burden.

I remember telling my mom a couple of days before that I

wouldn't have minded being in the hospital so that she would not have to take care of me so much. I was sitting on the couch just thinking when all of a sudden I couldn't breathe so well. "Let's get out of the house," I urged. "I need some fresh air." After I rode my grandma's shoulder to the car (she volunteered it every second of the day) we rode out. At first we were just riding wherever, and just because. But when I rolled down my window something happened. A breeze hit my face. It was coming from the north. I closed my eyes and leaned my face closer to the window. "Are you O.K.?" my mom asked. I did not answer, I just let the wind hit my face. It felt like God was touching my face and saying I love you Elise. My mom sat back and understood what was going on. Tears started to fill my eyes. I couldn't hold it in anymore. I began to weep and cry out. "I don't know what's going on Lord but I am hurting. Please help me. I thank you for heling me. I already know you are going to heal me. Please help me Lord."

The window was still down and I asked my mom to go on the highway so that I could get a good gust of wind. She loved the idea. My grandma was in the backseat enjoying the ride even more than me. "Yes Rosa, let's go. This is good for us." She was referring to spending family time.

Lately I had been extremely distant from everyone. We had a family gathering a few weeks before and all I wanted to do was stay in bed. It felt good to sleep and rest so that is what my days consisted of. Some days I would wake up, eat, go back to bed, wake up for lunch, go back to bed and do the same for dinner. "I'm sore." I would mope. "You still need to get out of bed sweetie." My mom was concerned I think when she saw that I stopped going to the gym. She knew I was struggling. Because anyone that knows me knows that I love working out.

"You want some ice cream?" My day dream got interrupted. We had rode all the way to Belton with the windows down, and now we were on our back to Killeen. I began to cry out again and thank God for still being alive and being able to breathe and being able to eat and all the things he had done for me in my life. Mom and grandma cheered me on and shouted, "Yes Lord." Those were the first times I had ever called out to God in front of anyone. I had been a very secretive, to myself, person all my life.

We stopped at a Dairy Queen, and got some cones and headed for home. We were having such a grand time we even decided to get some quick rentals. Though we weren't with the rest of the family, we were liking our 4th of July so far. When we got home we took off our hats and plopped on the couch. We ate some leftovers from the previous day. I remember corn and coconut and rice. Yum. Yum. And wings. I remember wings. We feasted and laughed and loved one another.

The movie I picked was two violent so we took it out. Grandma couldn't handle people chopping off limbs. I agreed with a laugh. When we were all good and full we dozed off right where we sat. For a couple of hours we were as still and frozen as dry ice. But I started to feel pain and I didn't want anyone to see my faith shrink. When in pain my positivity shriveled up like prunes and all faithful, diligent thoughts were flushed out. Not the type of cleansing my soul needed. I went to my room and closed the door. There was an invisible sign on my door that said KEEP OUT! They knew it was there.

That night pain turned into restrictions. I could not move my arms as far as I usually could. My movements became very slow and stiff. There were fears of me falling in the tub because of my lack of strength. My mom bathed me that night. First time my mom had seen me naked since I was a little girl. "Mom don't look!" "Girl hush. I used to wash that bottom when you were a little girl." "Well!" I was being stubborn knowing good and well I wasn't strong enough to wash my entire body. I could take care of everything. I just needed her to wash my back. It hurt when I tried to reach back there. I had to hold onto her shoulders to get out of the tub.

This is ridiculous I thought. Can't even take care of myself. If I was in the hospital, I wouldn't be stressing my mom out. She always pleaded to me that she did not mind helping me but I did not like being so helpless. I felt like I was a burden. I headed towards my room and got halfway there and I was dead tired. I kneeled to the floor and began to crawl. "Stop sweetie." My grandma did not like seeing me crawl. I told her I was too tired to walk. As I crawled into bed, I ran the whole day through my mind followed by some very deep breaths. What could happen next? Why was this happening to me of all people? I just did not understand.

Take a Moment: *There are some trials that we are not supposed to try and endure alone. Period. Find a meditation place and be around people that want to be around you.*

7

Emergency Room

It was July 5th and something had me nervous. Couple weeks back when I had went to the urgent care clinic, I got some meds. One of the medicines I got was for the neuro pain I had been having in my feet. The doc told me after taking it for a week if the pain did not subside, then I could start taking double the dose he recommended. So a couple days before, I finally decided to take a double dose. The next day was July 4th, the day that I fell. And the weakness I felt in my body after that point made my worry. I called my primary doctor's office but he was not there. I mean needing help to get in and out the tub was weird right? I didn't remember seeing that on the list of complications for Lupus.

It was around noon when my cell rang. It was the nurse from the clinic. "Hey Ms. Kea, I got your message is there anything I can help you with? Your doctor is not in at the moment" "No mam, I'll call back another day." "Are you sure, I can help you with any question or refer them to him." I explained to her about the drastic change in my strength level in the past weeks. I also told her about how I took a double dose of my medicine and that I was scared it was having a very negative effect on me. "Those don't sound like any side effects of that medication. Something else may be going on." "Well I did fall yesterday." I could hear her take a deep breathe. "Yes mam Ms. Kea you need to go to the emergency room. You should have went yesterday." She kept talking but I rushed her off the phone. "Oh boy....Mama!"

I told her about what the nurse said and in 5 minutes we were out the door. Special thanks to my grandmother because the past couple days she kept telling me to call in and tell the doctor what was going on with me. I kept waiting and holding off, but that day she asked me to call again. And I did.

We were on I-35 headed to the emergency room and my nerves were super bad. So many possibilities were crossing my mind. Am I dying? Am I going to be crippled? Are they going to have to take out some organs? I don't know if my mom and grandma were nervous too, but they sounded calm. "Everything is going to be O.K." I hoped so.

When we arrived I got into a wheel chair because of my frailness. It felt like we were in that waiting room forever. "Ms. Kea?" Finally! We went to the back and they performed some blood tests and urine tests. A doctor entered the room and examined my limitations while asking questions. Questions the people out front had already asked me. "What seems to be going on with you Ms. Kea?" As I told him about my episodes of weakness and Lupus, he suggested a lot of possible occurrences, but said he was not sure. We had to wait on the lab results. One of the things he said it could be was some kind of disease with my back. I forgot what it was called. But he needed to perform a test where he, he umm, examined my rear end. Let's just say that. I glared outside of my room, and my grandma had that

I'll throw my cane at him look on her face. Luckily he was handsome. I think that the only reason he survived. Handsome or not though she was lurking. My grandma don't play that.

The blood tests came back and he was just as puzzled as we were. It was not the disease he suspected, but my symptoms and muscle weakness was very alarming. "Well Ms. Kea, we are going to figure why you are having this sudden weakness. The good news is we tested for spinal diseases and injury and those results came back negative. "We are going to go ahead and admit you." I had to have a convo with myself. Alright Elise, you got it, you're good. Think on good things and just relax. "Can I eat now?" I had been in the downstairs room for hours waiting for my tests to come back. I had to fast for them, and I already had not ate since morning. "No, I'm sorry. We need to take a couple more test and we are going to need you to fast for those as well." Noooooo.

Along with that, the hospital was at full capacity so I had to wait on a room. News of me being taken to the emergency room had reached my brothers and their families. "How are you doing baby sis?" My oldest brother had recently moved to the Dallas area. He called to check up on me, but I told him I was doing fine, just trying to make sure everything was functioning properly.

My 2nd oldest Carlos came down with his family. Only two could be in the room with me at a time, so my mom and grandma went out to sit with the kids while they came in and sat with me. He and his wife kept me comfortable for a while. My sister-in-law Mo has the type of laugh that can make you laugh along with her. We were joking about how I couldn't eat. I told them that we should just get up and leave so that I could go eat. I was ready to go. Being in the hospital did not seem so pleasing anymore. Carlos told me about some lemon swabs that you can ask for to suck on. I asked the nurse to bring a pack of them. I sucked all the juice out the swabs and then started chewing on them. They found it so hilarious but I was so serious.

Finally after a few more hours a patient escort came to take me to my room. My grandma and mom were back with me now. On the way to the room, the escort, my mom and I had good conversation. I was complaining to him that I hadn't ate since morning. "Oh really yes mam, well I was just talking to a patient on the second floor that hasn't ate in a week." I got the point loud and clear. I looked up at him and shook my head. "Daaaang". He nodded in agreement, "I know right". Well it wouldn't be that long for me. Soon as they found out what was wrong with me I was "outty 3000." That night was similar to my previous nights. I slept on and off, but mostly stared at the ceiling.

The next day when I opened my eyes I saw my "ride or dies" by my bedside. I stretched out to see if I felt a little better. Nope. Not at all. I rubbed on my legs to make sure they were still there. It took all the strength in me to just lift them up in the bed. It was a pretty lazy morning. We just stayed in the room, ate and watched TV.

By the middle of the day the doctor came in with my lab results. High blood pressure: negative. Leukemia: negative. All the results were negative. "Since all the lab results came back negative we are going to perform a different kind of test. It is called a Spinal Tap." My mind wondered after those two words. "Umm and what is that?" "It is a test where we will place a needle near your spine where there should be some liquid. We will test that liquid."

My mom just looked at me anticipating an exaggerated reaction, but I calmly said OK. Inside my head I was afraid for my life. "OK so when do you plan on taking this test?" "Right now." Pause. Stop. Wait. Hold on, what? Those words ran through my head but I didn't say a word. He carefully explained. Another man walked in. "This is my assistant. I will put you in the position I need you in and then he will insert the needle in as exact location. Now when I do this you have to remain completely still. Sound good?" I nodded. I had to keep my neck bent over, chin touching my chest, chest at a 45 degree angle with my legs that were sitting over bed.

We made my grandma get out because I said she would make me nervous. Sorry grandma. She treated me like her baby, so sometimes I acted like a baby in front of her. My mom stood in front of me and told me to concentrate on her. It was quick and easy but the waiting period leading up to the insertion was ridiculously daunting.

Mentally I felt pretty good given the fact that I was usually terrified of any medical equipment. I hated giving blood, getting shots, the dentist office, and etc. But so far I hadn't freaked out or just had any type of anxiety attack. My nurse for the afternoon was a slender guy. He was really friendly and found me hilarious. So I kept entertaining him with jokes. By the time he became my nurse, my legs had reached severe weakness and I needed to be lifted by my underarm shoulders area. Whenever I needed to use the bedside commode I would joke with him. "Don't you need help?" He would look at me like I was insane and laugh. Later on I found out why he looked at me that way.

In the months after school let out I had lost more weight than I realized and was getting skinnier by the second. I probably looked like a toothpick to him. The very next day the same two doctors paid me a visit. "Well Ms. Kea, as you know, we tested your spinal fluid. The symptoms you have been having were compatible with a number of issues, but we tested it specifically for something known as Guillain-Barre Syndrome. Have you ever heard of it?" "No sir." "Well it starts in your toes. It begins as neuro pain." I had been having that pain for months now. I knew that couldn't be what was affecting my strength. He continued, "Then it works its way up. Now we looked in your file and we saw that a couple of days ago you were able to walk at least some. And now your legs are completely weak and you need help to stand. This tells us that the GB is moving very fast. And what we don't want is for you to get sick in this hospital or for your lungs to be affected. So we have some suggestions for treatment."

Doctors and nurses had been warning me not to get sick since I got there. They explained that cold rooms, weak respiratory systems and simply staying in bed often lead to pneumonia. In the past weeks I had experienced some type of heat sensation in the atmosphere that felt like 100 degrees and caused me to sweat bullets. I would tell my mom, "It's hot, it's hot." The air conditioner would be on full blast yet I would feel like I was on fire. My nerves were acting up.

The doctor continued with his suggestions. "There are 2 common treatment we use for conditions like this. The first is IVIG." Which means Intravenous Immune Globulin; it is a sterile solution of concentrated antibodies extracted from healthy donors which is administered into a vein. It is used to treat disorders of the immune system or to boost immune response to serious illness. (1) "The other treatment is called Plasmapheresis." It is a blood purification procedure used to treat several autoimmune diseases. "Your disease causes your immune system to attack the body with antibodies.

Plasmapheresis is used to remove antibodies from the blood stream preventing them from attacking targets;" (4)

"How will you get the plasma out? " I asked. He motioned at his neck and pointed to a direct spot below my ear line. I shook my head erratically. He chuckled, "During Plasmapheresis we would insert a tube into a central vein preferably your jugular located on the side of your neck." I quickly responded, "No, I think I'm just going to try IVIG, it should work right? The doctor nodded. "It should. We have not seen lots of cases of GB, but in the ones we have studied one of the two of these treatments usually works."

My mind was made up, now convincing the rest of my family would be the tough part. My mom and grandma were tired of seeing me like that and just wanted whatever I wanted, so they had no objections. IVIG is a pretty simple procedure. Put an IV in one arm and the IVIG in the other. Let it run for about 3 to 5 hours for 5 days. My aunt who was a director upstairs, she came to see me often and I needed it. When she came she would toughen me up. "Eat your food Le Le" (my family nickname). She and my mom are the toughest women I know, so when she came I would try to act resilient. I wouldn't close my eyes on injections or ask too many questions.

I remember when I was a kid. I would always try to be like her. She used to live all the way in Houston and I would beg my mom to go there and I thought she was a billionaire because she carried herself like one. I really liked asking her for advice about medical stuff before I asked other family members because she had been working in the medical field for so long. "OK Aunty, so what do you think? Should I get it? You know, IVIG, or should I wait a little bit longer and see if whatever is going on will run its course?"

"What do you want to do?" I shrugged my shoulders because I did not know what I wanted other than to be healed. "Would you do it?" I asked her. She looked me straight into my eyes. Yes." "OK then I want it." I told my mom. I would have to be taken to a different room on a different floor where special nurses would administer the IVIG.

The next day they found a room on the 2nd floor. Not only did I have 2 nurses but I also had a chaperone that watched me through the night. My nurses were funny characters. Very friendly, entertaining, and inspiring. They reminded me of the Olsen twins because they were always in unison and finished each other thoughts. Plus they looked like twins. You could tell they were friends. I felt very safe.

The day my IVIG was scheduled was the same day all my family came to support. I was tense. Being the baby of the family, my brothers were very protective of me. In my head I wanted to get the IVIG before they came but after talking with my mom, us all discussing it as a family was best. That morning my heart was very heavy. It felt like it split in two and I broke down crying to my nurses. I expressed my concern about my family coming and how I did not want to worry everyone.

By this time it had been nearly a week and weakness in my legs had maximized to not only not being able to stand on my own, but less movement period. My upper limbs were not being affected. Yes we would be considering as a family what was best for me but I knew it was either take a leap of faith or lie there till my demise. I was losing strength by the second. Paralysis?

Take a Moment: *Ever felt defeated before you were defeated? Then you still had to pretend that you believed you could win. It is* *not about the fact of if you or your trial is stronger. It is about be-lieving. Ever danced out of your clothes like David? When praises go up blessings come down.*

8

Conference Room

Everybody thinks their family is so different. That's why I just knew the doctor had never seen the amount of questions that he was going to face that day. But he handled it fine. I would constantly make jokes and apologize for my family's frankness, and he just laughed it off and assured me he understood.

When they arrived and circled around me it felt like a church meeting. They were all dressed nice like a big business deal was about to go down. Before the doctor had walked in and began conversing we prayed and I basically just told them how I felt. "I need this IVIG yall. I'm getting weaker every day. They told me the statistics and it's a good chance it will help me." My family was for whatever was best for me, but the question that was on their minds was, "What if it does not work?"

One of my brothers was an avid believer in the idea that sometimes hospitals make you sicker. "You don't want to start putting all this stuff in your body and make it worse." I agreed but I did not like the state that I was in. Minimal movement was not my cup of tea. I can't see how people sit at desks all day or stick to the couch for days. I just wanted an answer.

Everyone was present except my dad. He had left after my birthday and thought everything was O.K. Now this happened and he was coming from N.C. headed back my way. My sister-in-laws always gave my brothers the support they needed, but I think even they could tell no words could impede their worries. When the doctor arrived my family asked all the basic questions and got updated on the specifics of my condition and the steps that would need to be taken for my recovery.

After the meeting my brothers asked to speak to the doctor outside. My brothers are two God fearing men but I can't lie I thought they were going to jump on him. I gave my mom, grandma and sisters that look. We all just shook our heads. When they came back in they appeared not as uneasy, but still on guard.

The meeting was productive and everyone's questions were answered. "So how do you feel about this Le Le?" I was fine. At the time, no pain, no stress, just was tired of being in a hospital bed. "I'm ready, I want to get started today. I'm ready to get out of here." They laughed. I was tired of being carried to the bedside commode or having to use a bed pot. And I definitely did not enjoy all the needles and tests that had to be run.

As a family we reached agreement that I would get the IVIG. Two nurses would be present during the process just in case I had an allergic reaction. The Olsen twins came back in the room and started administering the medicine. That's what it was to me. Though it was antibodies from healthy donors, it appeared like simple medicine.

They cared for me as if I was one of their closest friends. "All right Ms. Kea, we are about to get started. "They inserted the IV in my vein and I let out a slight sigh. I just knew I was going to be out in a couple days. I missed basketball. I wanted to jump out of bed and go shoot some hoops. My family watched closely and asked a million questions like anyone who cares would. What's that? What's this? Is that supposed to look like that? Elise you OK? Nurse! Nurse! It was funny but I was so thankful for their support. Nurses would tell me stories about how certain patients never had visitors and missed their loved ones who were out of state or deceased. I felt bad. I felt lucky. I felt blessed. I believe the IVIG only ran for about 3 hours, then it was complete. I would have to get it 5 times.

Everybody was positive and believing in God that this challenge would pass away. We laughed and watched TV and movies all day and night. As each of my family left and gave me a hug and kiss we shared nothing but smiles. My first treatment was in the books and I felt optimistic. My mom stayed with me because she could see and feel the fear in my eyes. Mothers know their children.

One thing about the room on the 7th floor is that it was comfy. I couldn't believe how big it was. Too bad I couldn't walk around it. My bed was dead smack in the center of the room with a great view of the television. The hospital had standard cable and a channel for movies. This channel was like Redbox at home. It had all of the recent movies at the time. But I was not in the mood for movies. I just felt empty. I couldn't think straight, couldn't sleep or express much emotion. But something changed that, well temporarily.

The twins introduced me to my sit-in nurse. She would stay with me for 12 hours. So she would come in at 7 PM and leave at 7 AM in the morning. A healthy southern looking lady walked in and smiled. "How yall doing? Well Elise I'm going to be taking care of you for a while. I'll be with you throughout the night to help you with all your needs and we can talk, just look at me as a big sister." "Yea cause I don't have a big sister, but I always wanted one." I chuckled. She smiled. I looked over at my mom and gave her that "I like her" nod. She had to be in the room with me during the night because each regular nurse has 3 patients and in the circumstance she is with another patient and can't get to me, my sit-in nurse would be right by my side.

Though I was not in critical condition my status had the potential to change quickly. This sit-in nurse was so laid back but she also told me just like it was. Sometimes I didn't want to turn and she asked if I wanted bruises on my back from staying in the same position. I shook my head. "Come on then, let's get it done. It's for the best." The reason I didn't like turning was because it was so exhausting. The weaker I became the more doing simple things seemed like a hassle. The craziest fact was that I'd been told I was anemic yet I had to have the room 70 degrees or below. The heat made my body feel a certain type of way so we kept it cold in the room.

My sit-in nurse did her best to keep me comfortable. We would talk about my family and what I'm going to do when I get out. She even tried to help me with my constipation. The way that story goes is that I had gone for about two weeks and when I was admitted I begged for something that would help. So when I was downstairs they gave me a couple milliliters of some liquid that would supposedly break up my bowels. That did not work so I got desperate. The pain in my rectal area was overbearing. "We have one more thing we could try Ms. Kea but…" "Please, please, I have not gone in 2 weeks. I do not know what is going on. I can't take this anymore. It so uncomfortable." "OK, but what we will give you will make you have diarrhea and we can't give you anything to stop it. It will have to run its course on its own." I looked at them and popped my eyes like if there's nothing else please just give it to me. They did and the next morning I was told I would be moved to another room.

I ate a nice breakfast and grinned all morning expecting a great bowel movement on its way. I did not feel anything brewing until I saw the Olsen twins. It felt like a World War 3 was going on down there. I told them about what I had taken and why and they were enthused. "That's good Elise. At least you are not constipated anymore.' But I feel sorry for them. Oh boy I felt so sorry. I went and I went. They wiped me and changed the sheets and I went again. I had control of myself it was just I had not gone in 2 weeks. Like Cedric says on Johnson Family vacation. "14 days." So when it came it was on a mission.

By the time I could press the button and call the nurse it would come pouring like no mam I am not waiting. It was so embarrassing and I kept apologizing but they didn't mind changing me. I guess because I was nice. No it was because they liked their job and I was mighty grateful for that. So when I met my sit-in-nurse and the diarrhea had passed, I was satisfied. She helped me clean up a couple of times but when I became constipated again I did not say a word about any meds to break it up. I just sat and ignored the knot I felt building in my rectum. Laxative what? Oh no, no ma'am, no thank you, never again! I found that to be more fun than having to clean up a mess every 5 minutes. Better days ahead. Better days ahead I kept thinking.

I mean I wasn't hooked up too much. Just an IV in one arm and the IVIG tube in my other. I scanned through the movie list and my sit-in-nurse would tell me what she had seen and what she had heard about. *Twilight,* I planned on watching that. *Amazing Spiderman,* yep that'll be next. *The Lucky One,* got to watch a love story and get lost in someone else's happiness since nobody is coming to see me, in that way. No guy friend, no potential boo, no...." Have you ever seen Firelight?"

she broke my train of thought that I didn't want to think about anyway. "Umm no Ma'am," she hinted that it would catch me off guard referring to how good it was. I looked at the synopsis on the screen and told her I would check it out another day. I clicked on James Bond; *Skyfall*. I gushed the whole movie, I had liked him since *Cowboys and Aliens*.

With the light off and it freezing in there it seemed like I was really in the movies. The nurses knew what I liked – juices and warm blankets. I actually believe I shut the blanket closet down one day. They always told me, "I have your warm blankets Ms. Kea just like you like them." I felt spoiled and I couldn't help but to ask for another when it lost its heat. Movies, juice, and warm blankets. Honestly the meals were good, but I did not have much of an appetite. Plus I didn't want to get more constipated so sometimes I did not eat.

A couple of days passed and my sit-in nurse and I were really getting along. But its 7 AM and she has a family of her own so she hugged me, encouraged me, fussed at me and said she'll see me in the evening. My mom would always come in the morning when the sit-in left. There was a lot of areas to sit in my room but it was not fit for sleeping if you were a visitor; so most evenings she would go home and sleep and then come back. She would come back with stories about my dog, Maxine, and how she kept looking in rooms and searching the house for me.

Take a Moment: *Sometimes we do not like the suggestion to go talk to our family about our personal struggles. But, it helps. You will either figure out what to do or what not to do. And that depends on how your brain translates their advice or responses.*

9

Better....or Not?

It was about time for my last IVIG treatment when I was informed that I would be moved to another floor sometime soon. I would miss that room. I wished it was my real room. So spacey, nice television…wait snap out of it. Elise you have to get out of here. My night nurse assured me that she would come see me when she had time, but I knew how hard they were worked and the amount of time they got to rest, so I hoped that she wouldn't. I just wanted for her to remember me, that's all.

On my last night in the room I decided to give "Fireflight" a try. I was left in tears, motivated, and inspired. The way the story went was so realistic. Young girl driving accidentally hits a homeless man. She is in shock, freaking out and I believe she does not have a license. She drives off. This girl never got in trouble at school, was loved by her family, she just made a horrible judgement call. She gets caught or should I say discovered and is put in juvenile. Years later a younger girl caught robbing and stealing with her much older boyfriend is sent to juvi for not confessing and giving him up. So the hit and run girl sees the more needy and disturbed girl, takes her under her wing and after confirmation, failure and survival they both meet the requirement to get out. The first girl had such a positive outlook on life and knew how one bad decision could alter your future. Her positive thinking saved the next girls life. Positive thinking. Positive flow. Never quit, never stray. "Slow and steady wins the race," my grandma always says. I slept well that night. In the back of my mind I knew positive thinking and hope were my only options.

The next day after my final IVIG treatment, I was transferred to a lower floor. Again the nurses were everywhere and right there when I needed them. Ouch, another poke was needed. My last IV had clotted and had to be removed. The nurses said I was a tough stick. My veins barely showed and depending on the time of the day I had needed to be stuck multiple times. Darn! Darn! Darn! I hate needles. But every day, with every stick and every pain, I grew stronger. This room was much smaller. I required less attention so I guessed that I was doing much better. My aunt and mom were there daily. While mom would baby me, my aunt would call me just that and laugh. It wasn't a teasing laugh. I laughed right along with her. She was the hospital version of GI Jane. Tough and used to trials.

After two days in the new room, my lack of movement decreased. Yes! The IVIG was working. I would be out of there in no time. "Well Ms. Kea, the doctor said. "It appears like the IVIG is working. We were planning to move you to another room seeing that you are progressing." Another room? Well who cares, I'm getting better anyway. "Yes, that's fine." My mom looked at me. "Can it be a larger room because so many of her family comes to see her and there is not much room in here?" I should have known my mom was going to do that. "Sure," he replied.

When the doctor left my mom and I started thanking God and planning our next moves for when I was released. "Hey Ms. Karla!" In walked a familiar face. Wow, I did not even know that she worked at the hospital. "Hey baby girl I heard you were in here and I said let me come and see my girl." She had known me since I was 11 years old. I bonded with her daughter and followed her to the same AAU basketball team. Then we went to high school and played freshman and Varsity basketball together. Ms. Karla was the lead phlebotomist or supervisor of the Phlebotomist Department. In her department they drew blood.

She had heard through the grapevine that I was not doing so well. She would inform her church family, my previous church about what was going on. My mom and I attended Anderson Chapel for about ten years until she was appointed to be a pastor of her own church. I was in college when that happened so I did not attend either church for a while.

The day had come for me to change rooms and I could feel all my strength returning. It won't be long. It won't be long. It won't be long. Being transported by bed was a pretty fun process. It was like being pushed in a roller chair. A roller chair with pillows. They rolled my bed to my new, new, new room. I had met three sets of nurses because it was my third room in less than 3 weeks. The air was blasting, spacious and this television had movies and cable. Oh yea! Just for me. But after a couple days in that room I started going through changes. I would feel like the air was going through my skin and freezing my bones. Warm blankets became the best thing since basketball for me.

The nurses were very patient.

Daily, a few nurses would come in and check my cough and breathing. Turns out the longer you are in the hospital the more likely you are to get sick or catch pneumonia. That just sounded crazy to me. But I felt fine. "Ms. Kea, we are going to leave this breathing tool with you. It helps to strengthen your lungs. You blow in it and then you suck in the air three times. You should do this twice a day." I would try it felt like I had no energy. I did not leave the room and I was just so tired at all times. It was the type of tired that maybe an old person feels when they feel like they have lived their life.

My nieces and nephew came and sang songs to me and hugged and kissed me. They even made shirts to try and cheer me up. But my mom had to begin urging me to eat. Days later I had lost my appetite. Hmmm! Some changes were happening. The next morning I thought to myself there is no way you can get sick in 1 day. I started ignoring a lot of signs because that those symptoms would pass. "Elise guess who is here?" My mom's close ministry friends had come to check on me. Some more familiar faces that had seen me grow up and mature, entered the room.

"The Varnados" as my mom would call them were prayer warriors. They came to sit and usher in the spirit of prayer. As they sat and conversed with my mom I became very sleepy. I would dose off and wake up continuously. As I listened to the conversation I became dizzy. At times they seemed to be really close and at time it seemed like they were very distant. "You OK Elise?" I just nodded my head. Where are those breathing tools? I'm not feeling so well.

I had a scheduled x-ray for the day. The type that they do not do in the room. So maybe it was called something else. But they were very serious about it. About four nurses and another tech came in to roll me from my bed to a lower more mobile bed. They then transferred me to an empty room with a machine in the middle. They laid me on the table and instructed that I make no sudden movements. I could see a red line moving up and down my shaking body along with the machine. It was like those soda machines that have the bar that moves up and down. Whichever soda you chose, it collects it and then brings it down to the bottom. But you can see it happening. Yea, that probably does not make any sense.

Anyway, I could hear voices in a room in the corner. I guess they were reading the test as it went on. All that was on my mind was how cold it was and how the cold made it easy to stay still. Shoot I was frozen anyway. The only thing that was weird was that I knew that I was cold and my body felt stiff as a stick. Yet sweat dripped down my back and forehead. That was very strange. But I have some disease I had never heard of before so maybe it was not strange at all. When I returned to my designated room the Varnados had left.

Before I had been taken for tests they said some beautiful prayers and we called on God. They called on him a little bit more than me. Why was that? Guess I needed more to pray about. Ha! God plays no games when it comes to setting you straight. It is not the point that at that time I had not cursed him or gotten upset but it was the point that I had not thanked him enough. Maybe that's it.

My mom returned to the room a little after I did and we laughed and watched movies until the test results came back. Negative. Everything checked out as far as the Guillain-Barre affecting my chest cavity area. I'm laughing now because hospitals are one of the most helpful, miraculous places in the world, but they have nothing on God. How does nothing show up on the test but the next day I have trouble swallowing.

Spirits. There were spirits all over the place. There when I slept. There while I was awake. There when I was tested. Honestly they probably cornered me. Making building ailments invisible. Cornering me, but why? Why not let me get this taken care of God? Why the extra mile to prove a point? What point? Well I would wonder that for a while.

I felt so nasty and ugly. Being incontinent will do that to you. Though I could move my arms, my legs were still weak and I began to lose feeling down low. I mean I knew that I had to use it but I could not always control or hold it until a nurse got there. My aunt was a beauty queen expert so she promised she would get her friends daughter to come in and do my hair. She knew I felt a little out of it and was trying to help. Plus it would give me time to talk to a younger lady and encourage her a bit. Whew, I know it was tough for her to do my hair. When my bed set up tall only a person about 5 foot 10 could reach over it. She was only 5 feet even and had to reach up and around it to reach my head. She was so respectable and polite.

My hair has always been soft but the medication I was on made my hair somewhat like an infants. No one in my family could grip it. Not my mom, my aunt or any beautician. So when this young lady made my braids look so neat I was in shock. They were better than Alicia Keys....even neater than a young Shad Moss. I thanked her and wished her well. As she left I began to cough. The nurse brought my dinner tray but I was not that hungry. My mom urged me to eat. "You cannot fight a cold when you are weak baby." That was true. I tried to stuff down what I could but it seemed like the very sight of food filled up half of my tank. Plus with every meal a bottle of Ensure was included. After two sips of those things I was ready for a nap. Mom and aunt discussed my lack of an appetite.

It was time to do an administered breathing treatment, and what I got from the nurse's response was that I failed miserably. "You need to do this 3 times a day so that your lungs do not become any weaker," she instructed. "After every meal probably." But I was barely eating so this would be tough. As the days passed my cough became cluttered and mucus came up just about every time. Uh, oh I'm officially sick. Still had movement in my limbs but was so weak and tired. The breathing treatment that was supposed to strengthen my lungs became very gruesome and painful. A light blow begat a cough.

It was late and my aunt's god-daughter was in town. Very sweet girl. She was a freshmen in college and had plans to pledge in a sorority. We previously had great conversations about the pros and cons of pledging since I pledged in college too; social club that is. It was tough for her to see me that way. Before they came and saw me, they called and asked what snacks I would like. I cannot remember what the other snack was but all I was interested in was the Skittles. She and my aunt walked in with a bag of treats. How could I not eat nutritional foods that I needed to stay strong but want some Skittles? I have no idea but I was excited.

Skittle number 1 tasted delicious. Skittle number 2 was juicer and sweeter that the first. But as I ate the third and fourth skittle I had to clear my throat and drink some water. My mouth was dry and my throat felt like it was closing up. "You okay?" My mom stared at my reaction to the candy. "Yes, well it is kind of hard to swallow. Feels like my throat is closing up." "How long has this been happening?" asked my aunt. "Just now," I promised. We decided it probably was the size of the candy irritating my throat. I put the Skittles away and would save them for the next day.

When morning arrived, the doctors entered the room stern and with new developing information. "Good morning Ms. Kea. We heard about your coughing and sore throat from your night nurse. How is your body feeling?" Sometimes you feel like it is best to just tough it out. I grew up being taught cuts and wounds are battle scars. I love my two scars along my thighs that I got after surgery when I was six. Shoot, my mom believes in hot tea to ease a cold and as a family we were never big on pills. So every time a nurse would come in the room and ask how you do feel on a scare of 1 to 10? I would say a 5 or a 6 of course because I thought life was pain and that anything I was feeling was perfectly normal, seeing that I had this disease, that again, I HAD NEVER HEARD OF BEFORE. Along with some temporary paralysis that didn't ring a bell either. "I feel okay," I answered.

My mom always has the last word in a doctor and Elise conversation. How is that? Oh it's because she is the HMIC – Head Mother in Charge. I didn't mind she knew I sugar coated many things. "She is not swallowing that well and her cough is getting worse. She barely can grip a pen because she is so weak. I thought the IVIG was supposed to treat the Guillain-Barre Syndrome." The doctors took notes on what my mom said and began checking my eyes, my body temperature and they put in an order for another x-ray."

"Ms. Kea, from the symptoms you are showing, there is a chance that the Guillain-Barre rejected the IVIG treatment." I interrupted, "But my movement came back and you said in most cases it works." The doctor took a deep breath. He had a group of students in similar clothes standing behind him. Were they observing me? Because they sure were writing away. "In some cases," he spoke slowly, "In some cases we have to also try

Plasmapheresis." Oh no, there goes that term. Plasmapheresis is basically where they take plasma and separate from my cells because some of my plasma may contain antibodies that attack my immune system. A machine removes the affected plasma and replaces in or clean it. Sounds simple, right? Well the only problem that my mom and I had with the process was that a catheter needed to be placed in my most robust artery which could be beside my shoulder close to my neck area. We immediately shook our heads no. "That is kind of major isn't it? I think I will wait for this to pass because you before you did say before that it is possible for it to run its course and leave, right? And I mean I thought the IVIG was the answer?"

My mom asked for us to have time alone. We both shook our heads. No way, no how. I did not want that done to me. It was time for another family meeting. I wanted to make all of the decisions myself, but I couldn't see my appearance like those around me. I needed other perspectives. Just when I knew I would be out soon, this happens. But it will pass because my family is blessed, right God?

Take A Moment: *Sometimes positive thinking and hope are your only options.*

10

Can You Stand the Rain?

"Blessings on blessing on blessings. Look at my life, man that's lessons, on lessons, on lessons. "I like that verse by Big Sean. It speaks to the reality of good times and bad times. Sometimes you are fortunate and in other instances you have to learn from situations. You cannot go through life believing you will never get touched. I still ask questions when studying the book of Job. God told the devil to do what he wanted to him, but not to kill him. Before that Job was living the life. He was faithful, favored, and blessed. Well for many days I felt like the devil's punching bag.

Your brain sends signals to your body and if you are not feeling well, you do not dream well. That is one tricky system. How can you win if you do not have control of your body's ability to fight back? I had stopped eating and began finger testing everything the nurses brought in. And with the slightest touch of that liquid or piece of food to my throat, I began coughing emphatically. On this early morning all I could think of was not getting sick. The nurses had warned me and begged me to do my breathing treatment every day. They told me how likely I was to get pneumonia because of my weak immune system and the long stay in the hospital. So like a kid that never paid attention in class before a final exam. Like an unqualified candidate before an interview, I crammed.

I decided that on that day I would do my breathing treatment as many times as I could. 1, 2 3, 4 times total before lunch. Something was not feeling right though. I sounded like a broken whistle. I blew through the breathing machine and barely anything came out. I was deeply congested and short of breath. Dang... I failed the test and didn't get the job. Procrastination is the deadliest form of denial - Parkinsons.

My mom stared at me as I lay there almost breathless. I did not even want to use the restroom because I would have to be repositioned and it seemed like strenuous work. The nursed had already alerted the doctors about my rapid loss of strength. In came the crew dressed in their white coats. A different man stood with the group this time, and he led the conversation. He was not shy at all, so to this day my grandmother remembers his face. They both sat with me in the room when the coated angels arrived.

This new face among the doctors looked me in my eyes as the head doctor broke the news. "Ms. Kea we suspected that you would grow weaker because of the symptoms of Guillain-Barre, but because of this weakness, you likely are experiencing the onset of pneumonia." In my mind that just meant I was sick. "You can give me antibiotics for that, right?" The new face stepped forward. "Ms. Kea this is very serious. You can barely hold or grip anything, or constantly tired and not able to eat or swallow. Antibiotics alone will not do the job if you cannot breathe on your own. We really would like to try the Plasmapheresis. It sounds complicated, but it is a procedure that we are skilled at and are confident we will see results."

I hesitated to lean towards the idea, but like I said before I was not used to that kind of healing. I told the doctors I would take my chances and wait on the IVIG to take its full affect. It hadn't a week yet. I felt like it wasn't my choice anymore. I could only shake my head and look out at my mom. We both did not feel right about it. Isn't it crazy that your true innate feelings can be wrong? That you have the best intentions but you could be wrong. Just because you have never tried something before and you are still breathing, does not mean you are doing fine without it. And there was something I hadn't mentioned to my mom or the doctors. During the day it felt like someone was putting a pillow over my face and smothering me. "Ms. Kea", he interrupted my thoughts, "if the Guillain-Barre reaches your lungs as it seems like it is doing you will not be able to fight the pneumonia without being put on a ventilator."

Suddenly it began to rain and thunder with lightning flashing through the sky. I could see it through the closed blinds. "I have been having trouble breathing. I'm having trouble right now honestly. I'm just scared. This is happening so fast." I started coughing repeatedly and the doctors faces tightened. The new face grabbed my hand. "Do you want to die in your sleep?" He looked at my mother and I and she walked over to me. I no longer had strength to sign a consent for surgery. She would have to do it. We both shook our heads no. Of course we were not giving up, we just weren't going to go with any and everything.

A debate within the family was whether we were going to trust God or trust the doctors. In the family conference room, I thought we all decided that we would trust God to use the doctors for His glory. But you know people believe in God, but not in each other. That's why humans have so much conflict at times. We forget we were made in His image. And I didn't see his image until the head doctor held my hand and begged me to verbally consent to Plasmapheresis. He told me he wanted to pray for me, that God keep me safe, and that I not be afraid.

My mom felt a lot of pressure. My dad was not there yet and she was not sure about this procedure either. During the whole exchange of words. I began to grow weaker and weaken at a rapid pace. Talking became painful. I whispered to her, "Please sign the papers mom." She looked shocked. She knew I was tired mind, body and soul. "Are you sure Elise? Do you want to wait till you brother gets here?" She had called Carlos who was at work and told him how serious the doctors were. He was on his way but each second I got weaker. Wow, each minute I saw less clearly. "Mom, I don't know what's going on but I feel like I won't make it till morning."

Rain struck the windows of my room like rocks. It was early evening time and a sudden darkness fell over the entire room like it was midnight. She felt Him too. I could hear Him saying don't kill her, but watch her take the best you've got. I wanted no part in this demonstration. Bu there is nowhere to run when you are the only vessel for that venture. I nodded again and told her it would be okay. She looked at the man with the mighty prayer in his coat and let him know. "I am trusting you with my daughter" The doctors made immediate arrangement to have the plasmapheresis treatment start in a couple of hours. One problem…that quick the Guillain-Barre, was at my lungs and I could not breathe once they left.

My mother ran to let a nurse know and the last thing I remember was the voices between my brother, mother and doctor. The doctor's voice was Supreme. "We have to take her now." My other brother, Tony, was on his way and fear gripped me like never before because it was raining cats and dogs outside. Very dangerous weather to drive in, yet they were there quicker than a drop of a dime. Don't take me yet. I closed my eyes for moment…a couple moments…bright lights.

Take a Moment: *Do not procrastinate n life. In the majority of movies, the good guy gets there seconds before the bad guy gets to do his victory dance. That is not reality. Count surviving as a blessing and a lesson.*

11

Uncomfortable

There is no doubt in my mind that the doctor that asked me if I wanted to die in my sleep was an angel. He came and told me of dark plans and a plot to kill and destroy my life. I hesitated to heed his words and I grew weaker. When I finally recognized God's voice, the enemy tried to take me out, but at around 11 PM that night, I opened my eyes and saw my two brothers and mother and auntie. So many people have lost battles because of hesitation, yet He designed a plan for me to live.

I tried to smile but something was in between my mouth and throat. Something that stretched down to my lungs. My jaw felt a bit numb from a strap around my jaw and head that held a tube in place that was attached to an oxygen machine. Because of my delay in acceptance I now had to be on a ventilator and receive Plasmapheresis treatment. Or this was just His plan.

I posed for pictures with my expression never changing. Tony wanted to have a before and after photo. I couldn't see myself changing so he said that he would capture my growth on camera. Growth? Progress? He was sure I would get better.

Days without eating a full meal because of swallowing issues had left me hungry. Where's my tray? I know it was late, but I was hungry. "Have you ever had this protein drink before?" The nurse pointed. I nodded, I had drank something like it. Good, I was thirsty, so that drink would suffice. "You will be receiving this through an IV." Wait, What? I reached up and began trying to touch the tube inserted down my throat. I couldn't get to it. I only could feel the mask around my mouth and the straps. No eating? Drinking? At all? I do not like this test Lord. Did not like my chances at all. Not eating is like not breathing. Not true at all I know, but that is how I felt.

They say you cannot rush perfection, but I tried to get off of the ventilator in a week. I'm fine. I'm breathing fire. I feel fine now. If there is only one way to articulate something it is probably not true.

They took me off the ventilator. Ewe, that was an uncomfortable feeling. After the taped strap was removed from my face, the tube was slowly pulled from my throat, as I choked on it. Basically it was not pleasant. Ready to eat! "No your throat must adjust back before you can swallow again. Would you like some ice chips?" I nodded. Big mistake, I was not ready, neither was my throat. I gagged and choked up the ice chips. Mucus and cold from the pneumonia that was now in my lungs blocked my passage way. There was a particular way to get it out. Vacuum it out. Again very uncomfortable feeling.

"Alright Elise, we are going to try one more night but if this choking persists then we are going to have to put you back on the ventilator. I don't want you to choke on your saliva in your sleep. My family had been bringing burgers with fries, spaghetti, and all sorts of tasty meals into my room. I was ready to get a sample, but I couldn't until I ate ice chips correctly and x-rayed with cleared lungs. So I begged the nurse to vacuum as much mucus out as she could. She pulled out her tools which included a long straw-like tube that was connected to a small vacuum. She also had napkins under my chin just in case the sucking from the vacuum irritated my throat and I gagged. That happened often.

She would ask for me to take a break and try to get more out tomorrow, but I insisted that we keep going until it was unbearable. Finally when no more mucus was reachable, she said, "No... no more Ms. Kea," please take a break. I will see you tomorrow. Well it looked like it wasn't time for healing.

After a week or so, I felt very stagnant. Back on the ventilator with little movement in my upper and lower limbs. The way the hospital operated was simple. If you were declining you were monitored and assisted at the main branch. If you started to improve then you were moved to a smaller branch called CCH. Both places worked toward specific goals. My pneumonia had begun to leave and though I was on a ventilator, doctors and nurses saw improvement. So off I went. As I arrive to this smaller building all I heard was whispers. 'Wow! That's two Lupus patients. How old is the other? 30... They are so young. Yes, and this new patient has symptoms of Guillain-Barre. That is so uncommon, Lupus and Guillain-Barre. I have big ears and big eyes, so I can see things others cannot, and I hear through walls at times.

The nurses were very professional, but at times, my mom and I could see the pity in their eyes. "You look like a baby girl," they'd say and smile. That made me laugh. Shoot I'd heard that all my life. So many nurses and staff called me baby girl and looked after me. There not as many nurses and doctors coming through as at the main hospital. When the blinds were shut, it was very dark. Many days I watched TV shows and just looked at the walls. I missed two nurses from the main hospital that had really touched my heart. One African American woman and Caucasian male were called the dynamic duo. Well that's what I called them.

At the main hospital waking up to them was similar to waking up after a horrible day to breakfast and conversation. They were one. They took each other's constructive criticism and complimented each other. It was great to watch. Though they were only maybe 10 or more years older than me, they felt like my parents. When I did not want to follow the doctor's instructions, my mom would go tell them and say "Please talk to her," and one or both of them would come in. I'd just shake my head and I remember my female nurse of the duo would comfort me and tell me how tough I've been and how far I'd already come. "Let's move forward Elise. You want to get out of here right?" Then she would hug me. I missed her dearly.

To be honest, it was tough to stay positive. I had not seen outside since I had arrived in the ambulance. Had not touched a leaf or smelled the outside aroma. Because of the ventilator and mask that was strapped over my face, smell and taste were distant memories. My physical therapists did the best they could to help me with movement in my legs. There was a lady with short hair who reminded me of "M" (or "mom") off of the James Bond movies. Any older lady reminded me of "M". Anybody old and confident with short hair reminded me of her. But this lady was much younger. She had an assistant, and he would position himself behind me so I would not fall backwards. I had no balance or core strength to tip up straight. My new diagnosis was "atrophy." This is when tissue and muscles waste away because you are not using them. It is like they wither away or shrink.

As they pull me out of bed, I realized that it was the first time in a long time I'd seen my legs and feet. They were so skinny and boney. My skin was also pealing like it was dead. Anyways, they sat me up and we did our leg kicks and shoulder rolls. Every session after about 120 minutes we had to take a break. I would become short of breath and my heart rate would rise to 130. That is the heartrate of someone that is sprinting. After weeks of occurrences, the doctors informed me that the Lupus had caused heart arrhythmia, which made my heart beat too fast, too slow or irregularly at times. I took a deep breath, no biggy. "This is something I can deal with."

The therapy was very beneficial, and the family and I saw improvement over the next couple of weeks. I had movement in my hands and toes. So I felt free and like things were coming along slowly but surely. I could taste some Chinese food. I'm on my way I kept thinking. But the thing about being in a place is that whether your mind has surrendered to it or not, the atmosphere will engulf you, and circumstances will start to play a part in the outcome. I wasn't mobile so atrophy set in. Atrophy caused weakness in my chest cavity which caused weakness in my lungs. I constantly sweated in my sleep and woke up freezing. Boy that pneumonia came back like Jordan. "Oh you thought it was over?"

Yes, I had many conversations with my illnesses or sicknesses. I heard Guillain-Barre tell me I was not going to walk again. Heard Lupus tell me I was a freak and aha, you are not normal. I'll make you old fast. And my dreams were so negative, no wonder I sweated in my sleep. The devil was trying take me to his dwelling place. But God wouldn't let him. But why was He even letting him touch me? I started resenting God for that. Especially on this night when hope had started to show her face, but pain slammed the door on her. "Ms. Kea", thoughts interrupted again. "How are you doing this evening? We want to do a routine x-ray to make sure everything is coming along and the pneumonia is completely gone. But how have you been feeling?"

I see a new doctor every week it seems like. They have their rounds that they make at different locations. This week I was one of his rounds. He was short with glasses and dark brown hair. He stood confidently and smiled like he was trying to pass the confidence on to me. Simple x-ray results do not take too long at a smaller hospital. It was about 45 minutes, and he was back with a team. Not again! "Ms. Kea." No don't Ms. Kea me.

Take a Moment: *"Therefore I take pleasure in infirmities, in reproaches, in necessities, in persecutions, in distresses for Christ's sake; for when I am weak, them am I strong? 2 Corinthians 12:10.*

12

Pneumothorax

"Ms. Kea, we see a bit of air coming through your lungs. It is a very small hole and could have been caused by all of the coughing you experienced when you had pneumonia. We believe the pneumonia is still present and has worn down your lungs a bit due to the Guillain-Barre". Atmosphere, circumstances, outcome; Dang! "So what we want is to monitor it and hopefully it heals soon. If it does not and begins to grow larger then we will need to insert a tube between your ribs to remove the air that is coming through." He shook my hand and the team behind him followed him out while taking notes.

That's one thing about being a frog in a lab. There is no privacy. No place to go. I cannot shut my door and say do not disturb or I am having a very bad day. You must cooperate if you want help. The first instinct to be shy has to be thrown out because anything you withhold can come back and bite you good. I didn't have a good feeling about this. It wasn't storming and raining, but I felt him again, or so I thought. I heard something say you need to be alone.

I told my mother that I did not want any visitors that day.

And when my grandmother came in her place I asked her to turn off all the lights. I turned the television off and sat in silence. She asked if I was okay and I told her that I did not want to see any light. Where is my phone? I thought I had threw it in a bag on the way to the emergency room on July 5, and hadn't seen it since. It was dead and really the least of my worries, but I knew no one on the outside was aware of what was going on with me. Not many at least. I wanted a good friend to talk me out of my current mindset, because it was bad; all bad. Lord knows people need that collaboration with others to expand their thinking. But God was like no ma'am look at me. It's just me and you today. We had a lot of those days to come. My family would be in the room making me laugh and cry and suddenly I would drift off with him. Still I wanted no light in the room. I thought if I was lucky, I'd sleep my way to heaven. I hoped for it because I knew that the pain was far from over.

My grandmother is all about positivity and faith though. She kept hinting that a little bit of light would make me feel better. I did not want to tell her about the hole in my lungs because I did not want to frighten her. My Aunt SP was on her way over to check on me. I knew she would try to turn the lights on, but I planned to stand my ground. When she arrived she looked like she was walking into the Twilight Zone. "What in the world? Why is it so dark in here?" I just stared and tried to keep a serious face. My grandmother whispered to her, "She does not want any lights on. She is having a hard day." "No ma'am Elise, we are turning these lights on. You shouldn't be in here depressed." She walked over to the blinds and opened them. "What's wrong baby?" I stared and she asked again. Finally I cried out, "It keeps getting worse. Every other day it is something else. I thought I would be better by now, But it feels like this is going to last all summer." She encouraged me,

"Elise you are tough and there is no rush for your recovery. You're off work so you have all summer. It is going to be okay you just have to keep fighting. Do you really want to give up?" I'm not a quitter. Plenty, people know I'll fail, 1,000 times, but I won't quit. She was right. It was just that it was early August. A month had passed and I was still in a bed on a ventilator, helpless.

That evening the same doctor came in and confirmed that the hole had grown larger and the surgery could not be done at CCH. I would need to be taken to the main hospital. Hole had grown larger, huh? But I feel fi…., wait I can't breathe. In hours the ventilator went from my support, to my oxygen. My lungs were leaking out air at a steady pace. The next morning when I was being transported out of CCH, I couldn't help but panic and the nurses had to raise the ventilator oxygen level to 100% meaning I wasn't breathing on my own at all. Oxygen was being pumped into me. I needed to calm down but that was easier said than done.

From what I overheard my mom and grandmother would follow behind the ambulance, and when I reached the hospital I would be taken straight to the surgery room. Calm down for what? For you Lord? OK. I can do that if you stop letting him have his way. The insertion of the tube was a quick procedure. I did not remember a thing. When I opened my eyes, I felt drained. I'm sure that had a lot to do with the air that refused to stop escaping out of my lungs. My room had changed. Who knows why? I expected to have the same rom like I was SW's favorite patient.

Though I was happy to see the dynamic duo again, they were not happy to see me. Like I said before the main hospital was for patients who were not improving at a fast pace. So to leave CCH and go back to the main building meant I was going downhill again. Ms. L of the duo smiled at my weak eyes. "I'm so happy to see you, but sad that you're here." I nodded in agreement. I felt the same exact way. "That pneumonia is something else isn't it? She had a way of saying what everyone was thinking in a calmer manner. I giggled underneath my mask. She gave me another hug. "You are going to be just fine."

One thing about the dynamic duo is that because of our connection they checked on me hand and foot. I didn't say waited on me… they stayed close. I'd be seconds from a meltdown and in walked Ms. L. I'd have my arms folded shaking my head and my mom would be in back praying. Ms. L would look at me and show a sad face. She'd say my unhappiness affected her and she believed I was much stronger than my actions. She would just hold my hand and sing to me. I loved it. I would cry laughing when she would imitate her kids wanting all the expensive shoes and what she told them. She was sweet to my mom and won my grandmother's heart with all of the coffee she would bring her. Most importantly I felt safe with her and my family knew it. Ten sugars and four creamers. She even convinced my grandmother that that was a bit extreme and brought that number down to six and four. I found that hilarious.

Every morning I watched my grandmother pour the packets into her cup. I'd think "Have mercy," she is not playing around. My dad was in Texas for my kidney biopsy and Father's Day. Now he planned on driving back only a month later. I felt bad. Everybody had to put their priorities on hold because of me. Nobody minded, but I did. I wanted to be alone to rot at times. I didn't want anyone to suffer along with me. But they loved me. That's what people who care about you do. They stay with you through the storm. They are your umbrella.

PNEUMOTHORAX

The dynamic duo got spoiled by my dad when he arrived. My dad liked making people happy. He definitely was a believer that you are known by your deeds. Mr. R and Ms. L walked in still chewing. I gave them that "Really?" look and they began to express thanks for my dad and how giving he is. Come to find out he had bought donuts for the entire day crew. I'm not going to lie that was pretty impressive. Good stuff dad, they have to take care of me. I wanted some so bad and when they saw me attempt to lick my lips they stopped talking about it.

Moses Kea was sharp with his button up shirt, black gator shoes and "Morpheus" shades. A couple chains around his neck and a belt buckle to match. "I am so glad to be here honey." I expressed that I was sorry he had to drive back 20 hours. "Girl I wasn't going to leave you in here alone." I knew he knew I wasn't alone, but meant without him. We stayed up and watched movies all night. I didn't sleep well with that ventilator. I always felt like I could choke on it. So when I had visitors I would just watch them sleep and eat and laugh and leave. Darn, I wanted to leave.

The next morning my dad arrived with a brand new pair of shoes on his feet. They looked like bumblebee shoes. They were black, yellow and grey with white on the logo. My eyes widened as I watched him walk into the room. I signaled with my hands for him to get my communication system from the front of the room. This was one of the most stressful parts of my day. So to tell nurses and family how I am feeling, we used a flat mat-like keyboard. If I felt strong enough I pointed to the letters that I wanted so say. If my sentence happened to be longer than, I am thirsty" or "I need a doctor," then pointing to each letter would take at least half of an hour. Funny thing about it is I did not have to point to any letters to let him know

I liked the shoes.

I have big eyes and big ears, remember, so talking to me and my eyes not leaving his shoes made him ask, "Oh you like these?" I nodded repeatedly, hoping he would ask the right question again. "Yeah I got them from that shoe store by Best Buy. I just kept staring at his feet. Finally, I tried to talk through my mask. "I like those," I said in a level below a whisper. Talking through the mask was not a great thing, but it wasn't bad either. I only did it when I demanded to be heard. He smiled and told me he would get me a pair.

The next day he brought my pair and I couldn't wait to put them on. Ms. L had to break it to me gently. "Ms. Kea you cannot wear those until the swelling in your feet go down. I stared at my feet and the inflatable boots that were on them. My legs had been in the same stationary position for weeks and now my skin had begun to peel away as my toes and ankles swelled up.

My dad took the shoes out of the box so that I could see what they looked like in my size. "I'll take them home and you can get them when you get out." I shook my head no. I want them now. I needed something new and refreshing so I pointed for the nurse to put the shoes in the bed by my feet. I liked it when all of the nurses would come and compliment my sneakers. Even after they cleaned my sheets and changed them, they would put the shoes back at the corner of the bed. I actually felt happy. "Look at you," Ms. L. chuckled. "You have not stopped smiling."

PT & OT

My heart is beating so fast that I cannot hear the words that are coming out of her mouth. But I feel her hands guiding me to slide closer to my destination. But I don't want to go there. Though it is a place I have visited every morning and night for almost 24 years this place is not so welcoming. My legs have no feeling, but I can see them sliding closer and closer, and I am almost there.

Finally I feel the pressure and it is cold. I am frantic so they stand by my hips and in front of me. My feet have touched the floor and I have completed the first portion of my physical therapy. I am sweating drops that you could see your reflection because they want to take their hands off of my hips. Nothing was more frightening and difficult during physical therapy than sitting at the edge of the bed. "You are doing great Elise", my grandmother yet again was my cheerleader. "Do you know what I can hear right now?" I never made eye contact with my family during physical therapy because of my lack of ability to do two things at once.

Last time I took my eyes off of my body, I almost fell off the bed. Well the therapist said they had me but when you have no control over any movement in your body except for your head and shoulders, no one can tell you that you are not falling when you are getting dizzy. I nodded and smiled but kept my eyes on my legs and feet. "Elise you remind me of Rocky." Rocky would always fight to the end and find a way to come out on top. It was never pretty and he even doubted himself at times but he found motivation in something or someone; and that motivation powered him through.

So during every therapy session I pictured him running up those endless stairs. When I watched that movie as a kid I wondered gosh are they ever going to end. Then he would finally get to the top and instead of bending down and panting, he would celebrate. So after every physical therapy my grandma would refer to Rocky and my mom would play his theme music. I had the "Eye of the Tiger".

I remember my occupational therapist that came and brushed my teeth and washed my face. She was so sweet and reminded me of my cousin from North Carolina. Her hair was neatly braided and appeared to be styled by a professional. My facial expressions in the hospital were priceless. My mom and all of the other women in my family had tried countless times to style my hair but something was different about it. It was smoother, thinner, and very curly. It could not be braided so easily anymore. My mom had put me in headbands; grandmother gave me her head scarfs and hats; family tried to twist it. But none of it worked. My mom kind of felt bad about the way my hair was looking because every time someone tried to play in it, I pretended to cry. I needed help and fast.

My mom was quick to ask my therapist where she got her hair braided. "My sister braids it. She loves doing hair". My eyes lit up and so did my moms. The next day h7er sister was standing behind my "chair-bed" and she gripped my hair like a gymnast on the uneven bars. Ah, how sweet it was to not look like I had a Halloween costume on when the nurses walked in the room. No more scaring away guests. The mask over my face and weight-loss was scary enough. We did not want to add to the situation.

Take a Moment: *You know those people that are barely there in your life, but when they are it means a lot to you. Yep, you have that person's name on your tongue. Well tell them, they might not know.*

13

Angels and Demons

My high school coach came to visit as soon as she received the news that I was in the Intensive Care Unit. She was pretty speechless. The last time we had talked was when I broke down to her about my illness. She fought to hold back her tears and spoke with my mom privately. I believe it was the sight of me that was scary. As I lay in bed I looked at my arms and saw bones. There was no sign of fat or muscle, just bones and skin. The mask hooked up to the ventilator did not help. I still had the same smile so I thought, but it was weaker and not visible behind everything attached to me.

She hugged me, told me she loved me and said she'd be back as soon as she could. No more than maybe 3 days later she returned with two basketballs. One hailed supreme with its beautiful maroon and white rubber. I noticed that she had gotten kids from her team to sign the ball. She knew how much I loved anything maroon and white. A couple of days later teammates from my high school basketball days showed up with gifts.

I was in shock when D and Ash walked through the door

with Ms. Johnson. Now if you want to cheer someone up they are the crew to hire. That day I had been getting really hot, which was strange because of my anemia. So Ms. Johnson fanned me the entire time she was there while D and Ash told me jokes and conversed like we were not in a hospital. I needed that. I needed them at that moment. When they left I felt like things were starting to twist. They were twisting alright.

My dynamic duo were working in a couple of different rooms, but they finally came back to me. Never leave me again! That's what I was thinking. But I knew I had to share the love. Waking up each morning was an accomplishment in itself, but sleeping was very difficult. My sheets were soaked with sweat in the morning and Ms. L. changed them as soon as she recognized it.

Both my mom and dad were hanging with me on one particular morning when a doctor came by to check on me. He was a giant. He wanted to put a special tube called a pick-line inside of my shoulder area. I had been getting "poked" for a month now and drawing blood became more difficult for each technician. I had developed a reputation as a "tough-stick." Dr. Goliath, as I called him, told me the benefits of a pick-line. No more pokes plus medicine and fluid would be transferred through it. That sounded just like the Plasmapheresis tube. That process did not seem like it worked that well. They cleaned out my plasma every other day over the course of seven days and it was effective enough to get me sent to CCH but it wore off quickly when I began leaking air from my lungs. Time to consult the family doctor.

My aunt was not an actual doctor, but she knew everything they knew. When the doctors came to me with procedures they would like to try I gave my mom a certain look and she would say, "I'll call your aunt." My aunt worked on one of the top floors. She came as quickly as she could. "Hey baby, what's up?" My mom and I asked about the benefits of a pick-line. She was all in and recommended it as well. It would stop nurses from having to come in the middle of the night to draw blood and decrease all of the excess equipment that made it hard for me to be comfortable in bed. Her "okay?" was all I needed to hear. My nurse left a note when she clocked out informing Dr. Goliath that I wanted to have it done.

Ms. L and Mr. R walked in smiling. I was happy so see them because I had just used the restroom and at that time I only liked when they changed me. They worked so well when turning me that I felt no pain. A chest tube was in my lungs so movement was painful. After they cleaned up and rolled up my bed pad I started to feel really hot. This was alarming because my skin felt cold when my dad touched my arm." I'm burning up. I don't know where this is coming from." I started gripping the handle bars on the sides of the bed. The fiery sensation became unbearable.

"Mom…Dad, umm I'm on fire. I'm so hot, I'm so hot. Please take my socks off. Take the covers off of me. Please, please hurry." Ms. L put her hand on my chest. She looked at her partner and told him I was cold. "Elise baby we ae going to figure out what's going on." Mr. R. went to find a doctor, and I begged for them to take my gown off. But of course that was not an option. I continued to cry out. It felt like the room was melting. "I don't think I can take this…aah!! Help me, help me, please!"

My dad looked so hurt that he couldn't help me. My mom tried to comfort me but I just wanted ice. She and the duo put cold rags over my body, but it did not help. "I can't go on yall, I can't, I can't." My dad yelled at me to not let go. I began closing my eyes, and he started shaking me.

An x-ray confirmed that my right lung had collapsed and shriveled up like a prune. At the same time the doctors rushed into the room to suck the mucus out of my lung and allow it to begin healing, D was stopping by for another visit. She had brought Jackie, another high school teammate and AC my practical big sister when I was younger. But the doctors would not let them into the room. There was not much time before my left lung would give out. I could see them through the window doors, and all I could do was cry. They slowly turned and walked away. I shut off. This is ridiculous. There is no end to this is there God?

They numbed my throat and stuck a tube down my throat and vacuumed the mucus out of my lungs. The conversations that doctors have during procedures are pretty hilarious, but I was not in a joking mood. I completely understood their making light of things though. So much darkness is in ICU, they had to be the light. Even when my lungs collapsed again that night, they did not act defeated. But I didn't get it. Twice? Twice in a day.

I could not put my head around what was occurring. Almost everyone one of my visitors was praying for me or had put me on a prayer list at their place of worship. I knew people were talking to God for me. If I calculated all of my friends, my family, and my peers; and multiplied that number by the amount of people in their church or prayer circles; then that is hundreds maybe thousands of cries out to God. And I knew that I wanted to be healed. Was that not enough. That had to be one of the most unexplainable feelings that I had ever felt. Knowing that you are covered by the blood but still being sacrificed. That is what it felt like. But I felt the power of prayer like milk that strengthens an infant's bones.

Hate to say it but my mentality changed for a while after

that day. Even the dynamic duo couldn't make me smile like they used to. I told my mom that I did not want to see visitors for a while. But this time the family said no. I needed loved ones beside my whether I wanted them there or not. My dad kept telling me that my four aunts from North Carolina were near. I lay still and smirked. I must admit, there is nothing like "good country lovin." They arrived hours later. I was so weak from my deflated lung that I kept going in and out of deep sleep. But I saw them standing over me praying and praising God. I looked into those loving eyes that took care of me when I was a child. They placed a red prayer cloth under my pillow and claimed healing. I kept falling asleep so I do not remember them leaving.

I had many visitors the next couple of days. I thought it meant I didn't have long to live. The most stressful and heart-breaking feeling was not remembering when certain friends or family came. If I had been given medication or was feeling weak I had absolutely no memory of visitors that day. Guess I put all of my concentration into living to see another day. Like I had the final say in that. The next time I saw my high school coach, I told her that I was okay with it and was beginning to acccpt my fate. I just didn't know how my family would take it. She didn't want me talking like that. I think she talked to my middle school and freshman coaches because soon they visited. My old middle school coach came alone and gave me a good pep talk. You can't say no to her.

Even my first ever basketball coach, Ms. Richards and her daughter J came to see me. I had watched J play basketball when she was a senior and viewed her as a mentor. I was a grumpy mess. They saw that I sat in a room of silence for most of the day, so J bought me a radio and about 20 gospel CDs. Talking about setting the atmosphere, the CDs gave me chills.

They could tell I enjoyed it, plus my brother Tony was telling jokes and still picking on me. He cut me no slack. On several days my coaches, friends and family were all there at the same time. I needed each personality that was in the room for comfort.

I was tired of the ventilator because the tight mask made it hard for me to sleep. After a couple of days without proper sleep, the doctor recommended Ambien. All I knew is that it would help me to sleep so I asked for immediate trial. The nurse came in to change my mouth piece that was strapped to my face and attached to the straw tube that was down my throat. My sister-in-law spent the night and was talking to me.

As I listened to her, I completely forgot that the nurse was working on my mask. "All done." Huh? I looked at her and shook my head. I didn't remember her doing anything. She assured me she had finished and I blinked my eyes in denial. "What's wrong, Elise? My sister-in-law asked. Mo could tell I was loopy. I talked straight through my mask, which is really not supposed to happen. All they heard was air coming out. "It…is…loose." My mom asked the nurse to make sure it was tight. "Yes ma'am it is secured." I shook my head and tried to remember her tightening it up, but I could not. I started panicking and refusing to close my eyes. I didn't want to choke on it in my sleep. "It's loose. It's loose." I was air talking. "Umm ma'am", my mom did not look too happy. "What kind of medicine did you give her?"

Mo kept rubbing my back trying to sooth me to sleep. "Come on Elise get some rest." I looked at her with my eyes big and shook my head twice. She stepped out with my mom to talk to the nurse. I just knew she was thinking Elise done lost her mind. All of a sudden seven people walked in the room. I couldn't tell if they were nurses or doctors. Each had a note-pad and each asked a question. "How are you feeling? What is hurting you? What do you need?" I blinked and fell asleep for a couple of seconds and they had left. My mom came back in and Mo was calming her down.

"Who were those people that came in the room, ma?" She took a deep breath. "When baby?" I answered, "Just a second ago." Out she sprinted and Mo just kept calm, but I could tell they thought I was crazy. All I heard in the hallway was, "She has lost everything but her mind. I want her to keep that. Please do not give her anything else to make her sleep." I had asked for it so it was my fault. The next morning I had a wristband that read "Allergic to Ambien." I did not go to sleep that night or the next. Still couldn't stop thinking about those people. I saw them clear as day, and they were taking notes on my condition.

Take a Moment: *God is the most complex being we know. He can also make things simple, but His logic is so beyond our grasp. I get a headache when I try to comprehend some of the things he does. I believe those seven people were really angels. He wanted to test me and see if I would make my request known, right? You ever had that experience?*

14

Thanks for Your Help

My mother had been taking care of me since I got sick and now she needed help. She had lifted, bathed, fed, and comforted me. Being a teacher and pastor only made things more difficult. After finally reaching out for help, several of my coaches volunteered to sit by my side and even a mother of an old high school teammate came to help.

This visit was special because I was once best friends with her niece and she was a cancer survivor. She knew when to let me sulk; when to let me ball up in embarrassment. She knew when to tell me that I would make it. She'd say "I know you're hurting, I understand." And for the first time I felt like someone really did understand. I wanted to be a survivor like her. She was tough and really looked out for me while my mom was gone.

One day my feeding tube clogged up. I begged to go down to go down to surgery to have it inserted but feeding tubes do not require anesthesia. But I had a bad experience with feeding tubes previously. The tubes are inserted through your nose down your nostril and throat to your stomach. The last time a nurse tried to insert one, I choked on it. Given it was my fault because I did not follow her directions well, but no matter, I didn't plan on experiencing that again. And when I begged to not have it manually done, she called my mom, had her talk to the doctors, and would not let anyone try to put it in. She had my back.

The doctors knew I was already only 100 pounds so they wanted to hurry and fix my feeding tube. They agreed to numb me up before they put it in. By this time in my stay, I was scared of any and everything. I thought the ceiling would fall on me if I coughed the wrong way.

On days Ms. A was not there, Coach Rich would come and help. She'd fix my pillow and change the CD's. She liked the same shows that I liked so we watched television most of the day. Even my grandmother's spiritual daughter Mrs. Barbara came to sit in with me on a steady basis. It was not good for me to try and talk through my mask, so the nurses tightened it up, I couldn't whisper through it anymore. I really wanted to express my gratitude, but I couldn't so many days. I just lay mad at the world.

The paralysis was very inconsistent. On Monday I could move my arms and on Tuesday signs of improvement vanished. My waist down remained paralyzed and during physical therapy, three people were needed to sit me up in bed. I felt that since my body was inconsistent then my mind could be and should be as well. But it starts with your mind. Confidence and faith are seeds sowed that will eventually grow and bloom. Coach C helped sow that seed on a very special day.

It was about 9:30 AM when Coach C and Coach W arrived. They were excited to be there. I was confused as to why. I didn't expect anything spectacular to happen. Like I said my body was very inconsistent. For the past week, I hadn't moved anything from my shoulders down. Coach W was changing the channels and asked what I usually watched. I told her and she just shook her head like you are too old for that. I laughed inside. "Go to sleep, get some rest," they both looked at me. I motioned my mouth and said I couldn't. "Do you have any favorite scriptures?" Coach C looked prepared for a yes or a no. I shook my head.

I knew scriptures but did not have them memorized. She pulled two poster boards from under her chair along with a marker box. I laughed at her impeccable timing. Was this planned? What she did next changed the atmosphere. "I have two favorite scriptures", she began to write them down. "Be strong and courageous! Do not tremble or be dismayed, for the Lord your God is with you wherever you go, Joshua 1:9." Then she wrote on the next paper, "Be anxious for nothing but in everything by prayer and supplication with thanksgiving let your requests be made known to God, and the peace of God, which surpasses all comprehension shall guard your hearts and minds through Christ Jesus," Philippians 4:6-7.

She hung the scriptures up on the wall. Those were the only words posted in my room. I had been in the hospital for a month about two weeks and hadn't shunned the devil yet. I had accepted everything he had thrown at me. Not once did I rebuke him.

I repeated those words in my head. Be Strong. Be Courageous. Be Strong. Be Courageous, and my hand moved. Neither coach saw it at first. But I began shaking my head trying to get their attention, and finally they looked. I took a deep breath and moved my wrist again. When they walked in that morning, I couldn't move anything. I started doing something

I hadn't really done since I had been there. I started rejoicing and praising God. I told him no matter what else he threw at me, I would not give in. But just because you get better at something does not mean things do not get harder. Doesn't matter though, because the seed was planted.

"WIGGLE THOSE TOES"

There is a big difference between being able to walk and being able to move. When all of my muscles atrophied, it meant that I was much weaker. But for my legs it meant that I could not walk. When I could move my upper body and the Guillain-Barre had run its course, the doctors were worried about my inability to move my legs or toes. They ran test after test after test. The alternative I hated the most was acupuncture. It was more freaky than painful. Then when my nerves reached their limit and I was no longer relaxed, I felt the pokes. Freaky I tell you.

Anyways, I remember thinking to myself girl if you don't start moving you are going to be out of the hospital in a wheelchair. So I started thinking about Uma Thurman in Kill Bill Vol. 1. After her predicament she was in a coma for a couple of months. Because of being in a bed for that long without movement she was atrophied too. Well she was trying to get out of the hospital parking lot but only could move her arms. She made her way to the flamboyant getaway car in a wheelchair and was able to open the door and pull herself in. She had a dilemma; she could not drive because she had no movement in her lower body. She had to move her legs and adjust herself with her hands. So she was sitting in the back seat staring at her toes. She kept repeating herself, "Wiggle your big toe".

Yes she had atrophy but I also had peripheral neuropathy, or damaged nerves that cause weakness and pain in your hands and feet. Your peripheral nervous system sends information from your brain and spinal cord to the rest of your body. So somehow my lower body was not receiving these signals along with severe weakness. It took 13 hours of pure concentration for Uma to wiggle all of her toes, and both legs. The movie showed her stepping out of the backseat like she was brand new and stepping into the driver's side of the car.

I have to admit that there was not one day that I committed to hours of that task until I had those scriptures on my wall. Before then the doctors would stop by every morning and ask if I could wiggle my toes and I gave the same head shake with different facial expressions. That last head shake was the sad and slow one. "Make your request made known." That kept playing in my head over and over. Lord I want to move my toe. I'm not going to do anything but try to move my toe today.

I would tell my grandmother in my air whisper, "Grandma I'm going to move my toe today." "Alright now, let me see it!" she was so funny. Of course days passed and I hadn't moved my toes yet. You shouldn't expect the same circumstances and opportunity as everyone else. Yes that would be nice but too convenient. Especially for the warriors and survivors that make the U.S. thrive. Sometimes we look at others and say "Why are they not going through what I am going through?" I ask you, "Well how do you know? Or why does it matter? We are who we are. We must walk our own paths.

With that being said it took Uma 13 hours to get up and walk. It took me a week of talking to God and talking to those toes to see a twitch. As much as I wanted to complain about mental exhaustion and how far I still had to go, I realized that according to neuropathy I was not supposed to be able to send signals to my feel. But I made my requests known and it was a deep spiritual battle every day for a week. I stared at my feet and begin sweating. "Come on toe just wiggle for me." You see we have NO EARTHLY POWER but faith. When God sees our faith is strong he intervenes.

On the day I moved my big toe it felt like God's hand was at my back, so the wall had no choice but to fall. There was nothing special about my last attempt. It was about all the other attempts and never quitting. Spiritually, God did what He does every day and every hour. But physically the signal from my brain reached my feet because of dedication. Stay dedicated to what you do for your family, kids, community and God. You will reap good fruit.

Take a Moment: *Shout-out time! Okay, so my family held me down without a doubt.*

> *Grandma – would not leave the hospital and took notes when mom was gone.*
>
> *Mom – put me on her back basically. She never spoke defeat.*
>
> *Dad - put a smile on my face.*
>
> *Carlos – encouraged me to tough-it-out and was calm*
>
> *Tony – cracked jokes and entertained me*
>
> *Mo – made me laugh and took care of me.*
>
> *Chanda - also took care of me and made me smile.*
>
> *Aunt SP – was the voice of reason and gave great advice.*
>
> *My 4 Aunts – instrumental prayer cloth*
>
> *But the supporting cast with no blood connection were special as well.*
>
> *Coach Williams, Coach Richards, Ms. Angela, Jaquenta, Jasmine, Tay,*

WHY NOT ME?

*The Summerhills, Shantell, R.E.C. Staff, Brown Chapel,
Anderson*

*Chapel. Ms. Karla, The Vanardos, Coach Cannon, KKI,
Mrs. Barbara*

The Johnsons and Ashley

How many shout-outs have you made after you made it
through something? Do you acknowledge God and the people he
used? Or just God?

15

A Family Decision

A week had passed since the seed was planted, and I opened my eyes to pain on my right side. Because of the lack of movement the atrophy had increased, and my lungs were weaker than before. Another airway had opened, and it was twice as large as the first one. This meant I would need two chest tubes to allow the air to escape. These insertions were different than the first. These really hurt when I was turned in bed, and when I was changed. Any simple, sudden movements felt like strong pinches on my lungs. Be Strong. Be Courageous. Be Strong. Be Courageous. Let your requests be made known. God help me?

Life turned into the matrix. You take the blue pill, the story ends. You wake up in your bed and believe whatever you want to believe. You take the red pill, you stay in wonderland, and I show you how deep the rabbit hole goes. That is pretty much how my choices were presented to me.

My rheumatologist finally found me. Everything happened so fast when I got sick. She had been checking on me and collaborating with the other doctors on the medicines I could take, and doses of prednisone I needed to be on. I liked her a lot, because she was honest with me. My family were not her biggest fans. Not because of her, but because of the choice she presented.

She popped her head in the door, and I immediately expected a solution. She had the blue pill. "Girl you are tough. I heard about everything that has been transpiring, and I am happy you are still fighting. I've been talking to your doctors here and right now they only been treating your Guillain-Barre. We could boost your prednisone but that would conflict with your treatment for Guillain-Barre. There is something that could possibly treat both."

My mom had walked out to meet my aunt and get lunch. She walked into the room at the end of the conversation, but she didn't like the word "chemotherapy". My Rheumatologist was trying to give me an option out. She had explained that if things got any worse, this form of chemo would be the only thing that could treat it. Only thing is the side effects included reproductive issues and organ failure. Because of my Lupus, these chances doubled. But chemo would very likely reverse the temporary paralysis. After laying in that same position for weeks and weeks, it barely felt temporary.

Since I did not have a voice to speak, my mom delighted in speaking for me. I had signed a power of attorney form when my lungs collapsed. But she still let me make my own decisions as long as they didn't sound misguided. I was not leaning towards the chemo. Those scriptures really kept me believing and I was praying for a turn around. We didn't really talk about the chemo much because it seemed like a last resort. Give me my life but take away my world? I wasn't really feeling that.

Sadly patience wears thin pretty quickly. Days passed and I was tired of watching other people eat. Tired of laying in that same spot. My toes would not wiggle for me, and I lost my faith again. See days without sleeping felt like months.

I was out of it, and my family knew it when I wanted to use my communications system. Everyone knew that I hated that thing. So when my aunt walked in the room after having lunch with my mom, and I asked her to grab the keyboard she asked, "Are you okay?" I placed my eyes on the keyboard, and she started to run her fingers across the letters. I nodded on C...H...E... "Chemo?!" she exclaimed.

My mom had made up her mind that I shouldn't make that kind of decision without my brothers and the rest of the family. I just wanted some movement. To be able to stand on two feet would be more than enough of a blessing to last a lifetime.

I got a chance to see my KKI sisters from Texas College. About 15 of them came to see me and that helped take some of the load off my shoulders. They even kept my mom and grandmother company too.

Next, another teammate/friend from high school popped in. She brought her poetic CD and gave me encouraging words. After she left, more classmates of mine stopped by. Lord are you giving me a sign? Everyone is coming to see me. My two former teammates walked in with what seemed like a message in their heart. "Don't give up E. You got to keep fighting." One of them took a necklace from around their neck and put it around mine. "This necklace has kept a lot of people safe E. I gave it to my friend when she went overseas, and it brought her back safe. I know it will keep you." They hugged me tight and went on their way.

The necklace had a turtle on it. First thought that came to mind was something my grandmother always said to me. "Slow and steady wins the race." That was definitely a sign to have patience. Again, easier said than done, but I was willing to try. I finally agreed with my family that the Chemo was not the answer.

When that decision was made, a lot of the tension set-tled. Everyone wanted what was best and all of the talk about Chemotherapy was stressful on my brothers. They always pro-tected me and guided me through situations so the thoughts of not being able to change my situation did not give them comfort. But the way the family saw it is as long as that toxin was out of the question they could sit and talk in peace. Tony was a trial and error type, and Carlos was more so like, "No stay away from that." I understood both arguments. So I used other remedies to make me feel like I was improving.

I made tiny goals like holding my basketball in bed. I would read the names written neatly in permanent marker and imag-ine getting out of the hospital so I could meet them. Coach kept blushing over how much potential her freshmen class had. Yep, the thought of basketball kept me sane. I secretly plotted my return and planned for it to be epic. I would play basket-ball and yes the doctors were probably going to tell me to slow down, but slow down for what? I wanted to win the city league championship. That loss back in March was still fresh on my mind.

Another thought that was fresh on my mind was my kids that would miss me at the beginning of the school year. I knew they would ask about me and I missed them more than I had expected. I liked working with kids. No, I loved working with kids. I thought to myself I might as well be a teacher. I paused and smiled inside. I declared my fate in my heart. I am going to be a teacher! Making goals for myself was fun. I did not take it lightly that I had the chance.

Tony and his family traveled in from the Dallas area so

when they came into town they spent the night. The kids would go home with my mother and Tony and/or Chanda would stay with me and keep me company. Tony delighted in making people laugh. My ICU room was filled with snacks and candy that my coworkers had brought me.

My principal, AP, and my counselor had also came and helped out with goods. The school sent flowers and teddy bears to my room. Plus the 1st grade team that I worked with had put together a care package, and boy was it stacked. I licked my lips at the sight of it every morning. Those snacks sat right beside the autographed basketballs my coach gave me. The teacher who recommended me for the job in Nolanville even brought me a pink and white basketball. Three basketballs! I felt loved.

Anyways back to Tony Kea. In he walked with Chanda and the kids. They had a long trip and had not eaten. My nephew Jo and niece Niah showed me the beautiful cards they had made. They taped their colorful words of encouragement to my wall. My room began to actually look like "My room." "Lise can we get one of these bags of chips?" Tony pointed. I nodded and it was like a flash of light.

My two little nephews, Micah and Isaiah, flew across the room and then Tony got a hold of my beef jerky. He laughed and joked. "Lise, you know how we do." Those snacks were just collecting dust anyway. They were like trophies since I could not eat them so I didn't mind at all. Chanda smiled and shook her head. "Your brother is a trip."

All jokes were put aside when it was time for prayer. I liked it when my nurses stayed in the room or joined hands with my family. Tony reached by the bed and picked up a large anointing oil bottle. He but oil on my feet, hands, head and below my neck. I was covered in it, and the kids placed their hands on my legs and arms. Tony and Chanda placed their hands on my forehead and chest. I probably had the loudest room in the hallway. They prayed me to sleep.

When I opened my eyes back they were leaving with snacks in hand. They planned on giving my mom a break. She had been there every day almost. Tony spent the night and was knocked out like a bear. "Huh? Lise you good? You call me?" That is how he woke up. He was my bodyguard. I just laughed inside. The next night Chanda stayed and it was so peaceful when my sister-in-laws were there (Because I wasn't so ashamed when I needed to be changed. My sister-n-laws were not shy to help the nurses tend to me. It was a lot to do).

Chanda and I watched movies and talked till she fell asleep. Again, I did not really know what sleep was anymore. I'd last for maybe two hours, but nothing past that. A couple of night later, Carlos and Monekia spent the night.

I had the channel on outdoor natural sounds. This was hilarious to them. Drip, drop, drip, drop. Sounds of rain on leaves and water flowing in a river echoed from the TV. "This is supposed to help your sleep?" They giggled. I nodded yes and kept hoping. We sat there for a while and giggled at the sounds.

"Hey Le Le you remember this song?" They played an insurance commercial. I had seen the commercial plenty of times before. It was hilarious. It talked about humans being imperfect creatures living in a beautifully imperfect world. A woman opened her door by a business card and a car ran through her door. Then a guy was trying to squirt ketchup out of a bottle and squirted it all over his coworker. A man threw his old air conditioner system out the window and smashed someone's brand new car. The commercial stated "Sometimes the little things get us and sometimes there are not so little things. It's amazing we made it this far."

The video went on talking about making mistakes and how people are there to help us along the way. At the end, the song sang, "I'm only human born to make mistakes." I really was feeling that "message" at that moment. I could tell it was sent down from heaven. We began dancing to the tune. Every time it ended I asked Carlos to start it over. He played it back at least five times. I loved that the ministry was in the moment. Afterwards, Mo pulled up Martin Season 3 on her IPad. We laughed all night. I was exhausted from moving my head and trying to shake my hips. My lungs were a little weak from laughing. It felt like I had worked out and it was a pleasing feeling.

When I woke up, I wanted to change the way I treated the people around me. I had been a little hard on a couple of my nurses. When you are somewhere you do not want to be you start to get picky. Some of my nurses said that I was doing well for my situation, but I knew that I needed to have more of a loving heart and not take my frustration out on them. Over the next couple of weeks, a couple of nurses and I got really close.

While my family had been spending the night and fellow-shipping with me, an old friend continually came to visit me. Tony used to travel and support my AAU team that Coach Rich coached, so he knew her well. Since someone my age was there he was compelled to crack jokes but Jas just laughed and said she wasn't in it. My mom saw how relaxed I was to have someone my age sitting with me and called on her very often to come and sit with me. She was there almost every day for a week at one point. Amazing and selfless in her youth. I wanted some of her qualities. We all know of certain times that we could have put more effort into people or projects but we just DIDN'T FEEL LIKE IT.

So her being there with me, not checking her watch or acting stiff really put my heart at ease. Because I genuinely felt like everyone my age had forgotten about me. My phone was deep in an unknown abyss and I hadn't heard from anyone in what seemed like forever. But I knew that it was because of those tough nights of no sleep, long days of bad news, and mornings waking up realizing it wasn't a dream, that I felt so lonely. So yea I appreciated her being there.

If I was not initially thinking about the pain that I was in, then "Pain" would turn up the heat a little bit. It had to be acknowledged. So I was provided with what for a certain period of time became my best friend. "Ms. Kea are you ready for your Dilaudid?" My eyes would get big like I was at a Chinese Buffet. Nobody knew the high that medicine provided. I mean I was at a very low place. So to feel light, pain free, and actually be able to close my eyes and take a nap was a prayer answered.

But I began to misuse the narcotic and I certainly was close to addiction.

My aunt, as I previously explained, was a supervisor at this hospital and knew what could hinder me from getting better or prevent my other medications from working. "Ms. Kea what is your pain level? Is it a 7, 8, 9?" The nurse took notes before giving me my injection through my pick-line.

My aunt stood there and watched me. Dang, she had caught me. "Elise you know a 9 is like extreme pain, right?" I just stared and nodded like auntie I am paralyzed with tubes in my chest, what do you mean? But she didn't fall for that. "I understand you are in some pain, I know that, but I also know that you are tough. Dilaudid is no joke baby. You can get seriously addicted and there will be side effects. Then your process of healing will take longer and you will need to be weaned off of the medication. And this will be extremely hard, I promise.

So are you at a 9?"

She had to ruin it. But she was right. Whether I was high or not I was still in the hospital. I needed to improve, not just be okay. I shook my head no. She told the nurse I would not use Dilaudid unless I was in wrenching pain. I would have to tough it out. Fries have to have ketchup; drinks have to have ice; beds have to have pillows. I felt like I had to have that medication because I was sick.

But those things are just a plus to make us happier. We can survive without them. If I was serious about surviving it was going to have to be 2% of medicine and 98% of pure will and perseverance. So I stopped using that narcotic and took over the counter meds instead. Dang! Dang! But thank God.

The next day my friend Tay came by. She had me crying laughing for hours. She fussed at me for not telling her about my Lupus, then she cried with me about being in pain, then she told me a years' worth of stories. My mom was very excited to see her, she really enjoyed her. Tay was something else. She came to see me every time she got off from work early. One evening it was storming and she still made the drive. She had said she missed me. I was missed by someone.

She was ready to see me start moving again and had a friend who went through a similar trial. "She gave me a letter to give to you. Her name is Tammy. Would you like me to read it?" Someone who did not know me wrote me, wow. I was ready. She began reading...

Dear Elise,

I know you do not know me but I am writing you in hopes that I can deliver some words of encouragement. 3 years ago

I was hospitalized in S&W with an acute immune illness called ADE. It caused me to be hospitalized for 2 months (a week in ICU) and paralyzed for 6 months. When I finally got to the second hospital the paralysis reached me diaphragm.................I understand Lupus is also an autoimmune illness. I remember there were so many times I wanted to give up.....I also know it is one thing for those around you to say " you can pull through this, you will get better", but is totally different hearing it from another person who knows firsthand what you are going through and feeling. I remember wishing that I could talk to or hear from someone who had experienced this in order to give me that glimmer or hope that I couldn't find on my own. I am writing you because I am hoping I can give you that comfort I had hoped for. What you are going through is hard. Progress will feel like it's not much, but trust and believe that it is actually greater than what you feel. Even the slightest progression is one step closer to healing.....It is easy to feel defeated, but do not let yourself be defeated....."

~ Tammy

Tay continued to read and I couldn't believe this woman had wrote that much to me, a woman she had never met but felt like she knew. I was inspired to say the least. I felt like Maya Angelou had just gave me encouraging words. Tay left the letter with my mom and gave me a warm hug. The lady wrote five pages. Five! I was not only fighting for me, but for the next person; and it seemed like she knew that she hadn't survived only for her.

There were pretty stickers all over the letter. Well your light stuck to me. Thank you Tammy. God bless you.

A FAMILY DECISION

Take a Moment: *I am sure there is someone that you have been meaning to get in touch with but you just haven't had the time. Write down why you do not have the time and I bet you will be convicted to make that call. They need you!*

16

A Group Effort

When I became incontinent and could not control my bladder, I only wanted my mom to change my sheets and clean me. She would stay up most of the night with me just in case I couldn't sleep or needed to be changed. Then she would get up early in the morning and go to work, where she helped service students in the DAEP program at R.E.C.

I did not like to be seen so helpless by anyone other than her. Shameful was the word, and I couldn't help it. I became emotional and felt like I needed nurses that would relate to me and converse with me. I wanted a friend. There was a very nice but quiet nurse. I remember he was left handed. He came in and did his job and then left.

I missed Ms. L and Mr. R., but they were now working in a different part of the hospital. I had a bit more movement in my arms and I could slightly lift them up. Something that I hated with a passion was my belly shots. Because I had not walked in almost two months, nurses had to give me a shot in my belly so that I would not get a blood clot in my legs. My left-handed nurse would come in and give me an injection and leave. I told my mom that he wasn't that social and that I was already in a depressed state. I should have gotten to know him longer, but I wanted what I wanted.

We asked for a different nurse. Days later a veteran nurse came in to help turn me, and she wanted her intern to give me the belly injection. The intern happened to be a male, and he was a little nervous. Again, my mindset was straight survival mode and though daily I made spiritual improvements, I still feared that the walls could cave in at any moment.

He was very humble, but he happened to say, "I'm a little nervous" before he gave me my shot. I pulled my head back and tried to get away from him. Nervous? Oh no, he could stick me in the wrong place. I already hated the belly shots and now this happened. I shook my head repeatedly. He looked hurt. "You don't want me to give you the shot?" I shook my head no.

Well suddenly I had the reputation of not liking make nurses. That idea was ridiculous. What made things worse was that I still was on the ventilator and could not express my feelings. In walked the veteran nurse who was upset and let me know it. "Ma'am why can he not give you a shot? He is a nurse here like every other person, and he is going to give you a shot." I shook my head no. I could tell she had something pent up inside of her that she wanted to get off of her chest. "Ms. Kea, What do you have against male nurses?" What? Where did that come from? Yep I had a track record for not liking male nurses, or she'd heard. I had no idea who told her or how to react.

My grandmother sat on the other side of the room with her mouth wide open. She began to text my mom who was in Pelham, Texas on church business. I was so angry that I had the nurse spell out everything I wanted to say on my keypad. It took all of my energy and about thirty minute's time. He had told me that he was nervous and that freaked me out. I had her run across those letters on the keypad. That communication was taking too long. I forced my voice through the mask. "You should not have come at me that way. I understand you ae defending your protégé, but you are mistaken. I have been picky, but it is not because they are males."

That explanation took everything out of me. She saw that I was visibly tired and apologized. She asked if she could watch him give me the injection, and I nodded. I did not see them again after that. When my mom got back, she asked the supervisor to do an investigation, but my grandmother wanted me to forgive them and move on. I had used up all of my power explaining to the veteran nurse so I tanked. I told the supervisor never mind.

The exchange between the nurse, and I was needed. I needed to submit myself to good and stop thinking my way or the highway. There were a couple of young nurses my age that came through and painted my nails and gave me ice. When I had a mood swing, they would convince me that was okay. "Girl let it out. You shouldn't hold that in. I could only imagine how I would feel." I could hear the lyrics, "we're only human born to make mistakes."

Dr. Goliath was back from doing rounds at another unit and wanted to talk to me about my ventilator. He explained the benefits of another procedure called a tracheostomy. The ventilator would soon possibly bruise my vocal chords and ultimately damage my voice. The ventilator had already been used for an excessive amount of time. I smiled at him, I did not want to seem like the sad patient anymore. "I know you are having to do procedures left and right. Ms. Kea, I understand, but with a trach you can also talk when you cover up the hole. They would create an opening through my neck into my windpipe. They then could remove the gunk from my lungs with a tube they would stick down the hole.

"This will prevent further damage to your vocal chords Ms. Kea. It is a safe practice and when your lungs are healed you will have a tiny scar on your neck." At first, I contemplated but anything to get the straps off of my jaws was a step forward. I way okay with the idea, but my mom hadn't adjusted to all the cutting that was being done to me. I wasn't going to get the procedure done until she felt a little better about it. My aunt came and talked her into signing the consent. Aunt SP was my mom's right hand the whole step of the way. My grandma said that they had become inseparable. Tough times brings family together.

After I got the tracheostomy, I laughed and cried more. My daytime nurse was about forty with blond hair, and she liked having girl talk. My words came out in whispers. I could take the top off of the tube that was in my neck, but air would escape and I'd get tired. Just like with the ventilator, air was pumped into my lungs when I needed it, and mucus was sucked out.

My new day nurse, Ms. G was my new favorite. It seemed like she had done her research on me. Not like a nurse that read notes, but like someone that had read my entire biography. She asked questions, and my mom loved how she wouldn't let me pass on my PT. She believed in ROM or range of motion. She believed in progress. Every morning we would work on moving my limbs and switching positions in bed.

On the days that Ms. G came in, I had the same night nurse. She went to school with my brother and always brought me warm blankets. Sometimes I felt like a baby, and then I told myself, "You are one hundred pounds." While in the hospital you have to have short memory. I already had a catheter in place that allowed me to urinate into a bag. A certain nurse had tried to put a rectal tube in place, but I requested that she didn't.

My chest tubes had done their jobs well. The containers by my bed were filled with air and mucus from my lungs. The problem with the tubes is that when I had to be changed in bed, the shifting of my hips in bed pulled the tubes out. When a tube fell out prematurely, it would have to be put back in. And of course this news would come on a beautiful day. The effects of the Guillain-Barre were fading, and my lack of movement was no longer because of paralysis – but because of atrophy.

Carlos stopped by to see my progress and congratulated me on my new found movements. One of the lady Thoracic Surgeons walked in with her heels and white coat. "Hi Ms. Kea, how are you? I smiled big. "I'm great. I can move my toes, look." Wiggle, Wiggle. "Have you had any pain on your right side where your lung collapsed? I shook my head. I was already tired from our talking. "Well when we looked at your routine x-ray this morning. It showed a shifting of your chest tube. Two of your chest tubes are actually hanging out of your lungs." I put my hands on my head. The Kirk Franklin "Everyone Hurts" playing on my radio could not hold me back from anger, but it did keep me from quitting. The words serenaded my crying soul. I asked my brother to turn it up. *Everyone hurts, and goes through pain. Whatevers first, it feels the same. Be young or poor, old age or fame. Know this for sure, everyone hurts, we all feel pain. Everyone hurts, everyone falls. We let love in, still heartbreak calls. Tell me how much can my soul take. We make mistakes, we hurt we need amazing grace. So we pray tonight, that you don't get weak and please pray that I, don't forget what I believe. Cause these days are hard, and faith sometimes is work. Pray until He heals the hurt. I trust God will heal the hurt.* Chills flowed through me. *Everyone hurts but not for long. That weight you bare, will make you strong. Your guilty stains can be erased. The final price paid by His life amazing grace.* That song played as she spoke with us. That song played as she spoke with us! Thank you Lord.

My brother and mom asked for a clearer explanation. "So this is likely to happen when being moved in bed?" The doctor nodded and said she would send a specialist to pull the two stray tubes out.

I forced some strong words out. "She came in here like its nothing to her. Like she didn't even care." My brother reasoned with me. "Lise I don't think it is that she does not care. She cannot come in here breaking down. They have to keep their composure. She probably is used to seeing things like this happen." I understood perfectly; God use me. Five minutes later he came, and I lay there silent. A quick pinch and it was over. Ms. G tried to cheer me up the best she could.

The next day she was turning me in bed, and after she removed my sheets she stood alongside her team member (nurse) silent. "Are we almost done? I asked. "Yes," she whispered. I looked up and tried to find her face but no one was by my bed. Up popped Ms. G from the side of the bed with her partner. They gave me a very suspicious smile. I reached to my side. My last tube had fallen out.

Take a Moment: *"Watch therefore, for ye know neither the day nor the hour wherein the Son of man cometh." Matthew 25.13. Do you think he was only taking about his return? He was talking about being ready for blessings as well. Don't you think?*

17

Back and Forth

I freaked out. I mean I went off the deep end. Ms. G had to calm me down before I caused myself to have some sort of attack. "Elise! Elise! I didn't want to say anything because I did not want to scare you. But it came out clean. We did not pull it out. It slid out on its own. The doctor is on his way to look at it." I just stared at them until the Thoracic doctor arrived.

Thoughts of starting over crossed my mind. I will need more scriptures and more prayer if this process is prolonged. He kneeled at my bed and observed my right side with the nurses. I heard ah's and wow's. So of course, I tried to turn over. "We are going to order an x-ray to see what it looks like on the inside. I'll be back in a few."

I couldn't believe my ears when the Thoracic Unit all came into my room and informed me that the tubes had fallen out because the hole in my lungs had closed and healed. I apologized to Ms. G and her partner. Then I thanked the other nurse for taking care of me previous days as well. "What does this mean?" Ms. G smiled with confidence, "This means you are on your way out of here." If my lungs were healing, then soon

I would no longer need a trach. I would be able to eat and talk again.

That night things got really embarrassing. My grandmother was in the room with me and she said she smelled something. I needed to be cleaned again. This was the 3rd time in less than an hour and it was about one o'clock in the morning. An hour later, I'd gone four more times. The nurse was very frustrated, because I did not want a rectal tube. I'm sure she had other patients, and I was not easy to manage. You had to flip me and turn me, then clean me.

Though my arms could move and my toes did too, my core was my weakest point. I couldn't turn on my own and still needed assistance. There was no sleep for me that night or rest for any nurses. I had to be changed again and again and again. "I can't catch a break grandma. I do not understand. Every time things appear to get better trouble falls out of the sky."

My grandma wanted me to get one thing straight. "It is the enemy. He only comes to kill, steal, and destroy. What you said is that every time God blesses you, something bad happens. Then you have to be ready! Know that the devil is going to give you his best shot because he knows what God has for you! This means you are going to have a break through tomorrow. Just watch! He does not want for you to make it to tomorrow because if you do, he will be defeated."

She was right. S&W wanted to get a discharge date arranged, and order that I continue my care at CCH until my body was ready for rehab. The only reason my lower function was erratic was that I had no feeling and then I regained feeling. My body had loss its muscle memory of how to control itself. I did not know how to use the restroom on my own.

That next night, again I could not stop myself from going in the bed. Moments after being changed my feeding tube clogged up. My discharge date would be the following day, and if I waited to have the surgery center insert the tube back in in my nose, it would not be scheduled till the next day. The nurses used a Coke to try and unclog the tube, but it did not work.

My night nurse brought a tall red-haired young woman in the room. She told her that I did not want a rectal tube, and that I did not want the feeding tube put back in without being numb. "Ms. Kea you know they are not going to let you leave without a feeding tube. And if you keep using the restroom on yourself, you are going to get an infection." "But I am trying to hold it until you all get here."

She put her hand on my shoulder and smiles. "I know. I know you can't help it. You were paralyzed and lost your strength. You have no control of the muscle. So until you regain control, let me help you. Please let me help you." I grabbed her hand. "I am putting my trust in you. I had bad experiences with both tools so…I'm trusting you."

Tears rolled down my face and then she started to cry. I think she understood that I was just tired and I didn't want any more pain or setbacks. A break for just one night was on my mind. She told the other nurse to get the tools. She asked my grandmother to talk to me while she put them in. I didn't choke this time, and the tube wasn't unbearable. What was the difference? Trust? Trust! Wow!

I thanked her and thanked her some more. I will never forget crying with her. The next day they took the trach out of my neck and put a bandage over my hole. It would take about a month to close on its own. One by one doctors and nurses came to say farewell and told me they'd never forget me and would tell other patients about my recovery. I laughed thinking about the good stories and the bad. What a process! But it definitely was not over yet. It was hard saying goodbye to everyone but not that hard.

On August 27, 2013, I passed a swallow test. I got to say my goodbyes to the "Dynamic duo". Food was on my mind. News had finally made it to my entire city league team. The coach/player Shantell had come to check on me and said she would be spending a lot more time with me after I transferred. She was a joy to be around and my grandma loved her attitude so I was excited. After I passed the swallow exam, I was told I would start eating when I got to CCH. His grace is sufficient.

The ambulance ride was different than the other two rides I had taken. It felt very devotional. God shined a light into the ambulance and though there were not rainbows in the sky, I felt like one. I was now a representation of His mercy. It was no longer a test, but my job to be more transparent.

A week prior to my last day in the main hospital, I had more visits from teammates and basketball coaches. Jas had to try and find a new movie every day because I had watched every single film that was on the guide list. A doctor who I had never seen before was asked to stop by my room for a brief exam. After noting my weakness in my limbs, he asked how I felt. I was very motivated that day so I gave him the biggest smile.

"Alright Ms. Kea, well you have shown some improvement, but you still need to get a bit stronger. Have a good day, and I will see you in a couple of weeks." I looked at Jas and looked back at the doc and shook my head. He laughed, "I won't see you in a couple of weeks?" Again I shook my head. He giggled out of the room. "That's a good mindset to have."

He was not the devil, but I felt the enemy's presence when he laughed at me. He unintentionally delivered a message for him. The message was girl you are not going anywhere. So as I prayed and worshipped to myself in the ambulance, I reflected on my journey. I believe the process was extended because of my lack of faith. Shoot it could also have been drawn out simply because He wanted it to be. That is a possibility that I am perfectly comfortable with now.

I realized my fighting to survive was not for me to live but for Him to live. Him being God. I was in ICU for about a month and had surgeries and procedures left and right. Was there a lesson that I would learn? Maybe a reward? But God's way of thinking is not our way. We are clay in His hands. Maybe He wanted to put His spirit back into the ICU. Lord knows my family was not afraid to pray down walls.

Why didn't I perceive the occasions that interns surrounded my bed as chances to boast about God? I was told that my condition was very peculiar. I was the 3rd reported case of Lupus and Guillain-Barre at the same time…in history. That is what my kidney doctor told me. But why was God using me for this found study? It had only been about five months since I was diagnosed with SLE. But God allowed me time to become stronger and to humble myself.

As I sat in that ambulance, I realized that I was not my own. That I was a vessel and that I needed to willingly submit to God. We are not worthy, no matter how important we think we are. Life is a blessing and those couple of month's trials surely showed me that He could use anybody. He used so many people to touch my life during my stay at S&W.

After witnessing Him flip, change, and alter so many situations in my hospital room, I finally understood all I could ever have the power to do was throw my hands back and continue to pray "Thy will be done." So the Lord reconstructed certain parts of my insides and broke down my physical structure. Then he nodded and said, "NOW I CAN USE YOU."

Any opposition you are facing is just God's way of preparing you for a breakthrough.

But whatever you do, **don't watch the clock; do what it does. Keep going ~ Sam Levenson**

Acknowledgements

Thank you to my nieces and nephews for your smiles and maturity in such a confusing couple of months.

Thank you to the nurses who worked countless hours to make sure that I was comfortable, even in my pain.

Thank you to the doctors who quickly diagnosed me and studied my symptoms. Your constant effort toward finding an adequate treatment did not go unnoticed.

Thank you to all of my visitors that took time out of their busy schedule to come and see if I was okay.

Thank you to Unum, the Killeen Independent School District, and R.E.C. for approving and understanding my medical leave.

Thank you to the teachers, ministers, coaches, and colleagues that called and sent gifts.

Thank you to my college basketball coaches that prepared me for battle. The doctors informed me that if I was not in such great shape, I would have not made it. Pledging to a social club in college and conditioning for college basketball are the second two hardest obstacles I have ever faced.

ACKNOWLEDGEMENTS

Thank you to Brown Chapel and Anderson Chapels for your gifts and prayers.

And finally, thank you to my family: Mom, Dad, Grandma, Carlos, Tony, Monekia, Chanda, Aunt SP, Aunt Lavern, Aunt Joyce, Aunt Lula, Aunt Gardenia, Kyre, Jovaune, Denasia, Zaniah, Mya, Micah and Isaiah. You all prayed those hospital walls down. I love you and appreciate you all. Your time and dedication towards me was not required, but you made it a priority. Thank you grandma for never leaving my side. Muah!

What' Next?

Rehab for the Soul

A recollection of the process a young woman took to encompass the strength to stand and eat; her thoughts on unforgettable people she met at the Complete Care Hospital, and her transferring to the Texas Neuro Rehab where friends and family visited frequently. The love and care of the staff and a friendly patient with nothing to lose changed the way she viewed the word "**Struggle**."

Based off of my real life experience at Texas Nuero Rehab.

References

1. BDI Pharma, Inc. Feb 2009. BDI Pharma, Inc. Clinical Glossary. 15 May 2009. http://www.ddipharma.com/clinical-glossary-1.aspx.

2. Ruiz-Irastora G. Ramos- Casals M, Brito- Zeron P, Khamashta MA. Clinical efficacy and side effects of antimal arials in systemic lupus erythematosus: a systematic

review. Ann Rheum Dis. Zolo;69:20-28.[RubMed]

3. Russell, Shannon." Lauren Hill dies at 19 after battle with brain cancer." Cincinnati Enquirer. USA Today Sports. Contributing: The Associated Press.

4. Samuels, Martin, and Steven Feske, editors, Office Practice of Nuerology. New York: Churchhill Livingstone, 1996.

5. U.S. Census Bureau, International Data Base. http://www. census.gov/population/popwnotes.html

CPSIA information can be obtained
at www.ICGtesting.com
Printed in the USA
LVOW11s1453270617
539528LV00035B/22/P